Advance Praise for *The*

"Suspicious of institutionalism, ye   _al; seeking peace
and reconciliation, yet insensitive tc   _se many women face; valu-
ing self-giving love, yet celebrating materialism; the paradoxical nature
of the Twilight saga is helpfully explored in Elaine Heath's winsome
addition to the best-selling Gospel according To series. Here is a good
read for fans and inquirers alike."

Robert K. Johnston, author of *Reel Spirituality:*
Theology and Film in Dialogue and Professor of Theology
and Culture, Fuller Theological Seminary

"Eager to understand the Twilight phenomenon? Elaine Heath offers a
generous appreciation of its vision of a peaceable kingdom where vampires, werewolves, and humans cooperate. For Twi-hard fans, Heath also
offers a constructive critique of the gender roles and violence looming
beneath Twilight's shimmering surfaces. *The Gospel according to Twilight* is smart, accessible, and insightful."

Craig Detweiler, Center for Entertainment, Media,
and Culture, Pepperdine University

"Anyone interested in the power of popular culture to shape the hearts
and minds of the next generation ought to read Elaine Heath's *The Gospel according to Twilight: Women, Sex, and God*. Her critical reading of
the Twilight series through a Christian, feminist lens makes its positive
impact clear and accessible for readers of Twilight, pastors, preachers,
teachers, and parents. It also makes its negative impact clear and accessible. Heath, a theologian, evangelism professor, pastor, and self-described
"lover of good stories," does the Twilight saga justice at the same time
that she critiques its glamorization of gender stereotypes with their potential for violence and abuse. She portrays the positive themes of the book,
the ways in which sacrifice, redemption, social critique, justice, and compassion shine through its plot and characters. At the same time she shines
a critical light into what lurks in the shadows of Twilight: a glorification
of female submission and a seductive portrayal of sexual violence. To top
it all off, Heath writes with an elegance and edge that make her book as
much of a page-turner as the series on which it is based."

Alyce M. McKenzie, Professor of Homiletics,
Perkins School of Theology

"In this captivating work, Elaine Heath writes a sustained, theological reflection on the Twilight novels. Not content to merely celebrate or condemn Stephenie Meyer's stories in a simplistic manner, Heath understands the characters and the stories on their own terms before putting them in conversation with the gospel. Clearly, Heath has done her homework. On the critical side, Heath writes about the difficult portrayal women receive in Twilight and how these characters' actions are not consistent with the Christian life. But through compelling portraits of Bella, Edward, and the Cullens, she reveals what Twilight might positively reveal about family, desire, love, and self-sacrifice. Delving deeper into theological themes, she reflects on the Trinity, the kingdom of God, salvation, and finally eschatology, all within the world of Twilight. Her weaving of gospel themes within the Twilight story itself is inspiring and gives further insight both to the books and to a contemporary understanding of the gospel itself. This is an engaging, creative read that is timely for those looking to connect their faith to popular culture."

Ryan Bolger, Associate Professor of Church in
Contemporary Culture, Fuller Theological Seminary,
and coauthor of *Emerging Churches: Creating Christian
Community in Postmodern Cultures*

The Gospel according to Twilight

The Gospel according to Twilight

Women, Sex, and God

Elaine A. Heath

Published in the United States of America in 2011 by
Westminster John Knox Press, Louisville, Kentucky

First published in Great Britain in 2011

Society for Promoting Christian Knowledge
36 Causton Street
London SW1P 4ST
www.spckpublishing.co.uk

This book has not been prepared, endorsed or licensed by any person or entity
that created, published or produced the main characters, subjects or
related properties of the Twilight saga.

The author and publisher have made every effort to ensure that the external website
and email addresses included in this book are correct and up to date at the time
of going to press. The author and publisher are not responsible for the
content, quality or continuing accessibility of the sites.

Unless otherwise noted, Scripture quotations are taken from the New Revised
Standard Version of the Bible, copyright © 1989 by the Division of Christian
Education of the National Council of the Churches of Christ in the USA.
Used by permission. All rights reserved.

Scripture quotations marked NIV are from the HOLY BIBLE, NEW
INTERNATIONAL VERSION. Copyright © 1973, 1978, 1984 by
International Bible Society. Used by permission of Hodder &
Stoughton Publishers, a member of the Hachette UK Group.
All rights reserved. 'NIV' is a registered trademark of
International Bible Society.
UK trademark number 1448790.

British Library Cataloguing-in-Publication Data
A catalogue record for this book is available from the British Library

ISBN 978–0–281–06661–2
eBook ISBN 978–0–281–06662–9

First printed in Great Britain by Ashford Colour Press
Subsequently digitally printed in Great Britain

Produced on paper from sustainable forests

For Holly

Contents

Introduction

My daughter, an engineering graduate student, had scarcely gotten into the car with her suitcase when she thrust a book into my hands. *Twilight.*

"Mom, you should read this," she said.

"Vampires?" I asked. Really? I had better things to do over Christmas break, and I was tired.

"Seriously, you will love it," she insisted. I noticed the Eve motif in the cover art, with a young woman's hands emerging from the darkness, holding an apple.

"Tell me more," I said. I hadn't paid much attention to this book, although I had heard it was number one on the *New York Times* best-seller list. A movie had just come out, too. I flipped it over and skimmed the back cover. Maybe she was right. I was going to be teaching a course on the gospel and popular culture after Christmas break. Should I include something about *Twilight*?

When my other daughter arrived home for the holidays, a similar conversation took place. Over the next few days, their trips to the bookstore yielded the remaining three installments of the Twilight saga, which both daughters consumed eagerly. The books grew into a dark tower on the coffee table, generating comments from friends who came to visit. Everyone, it seemed, was reading these novels. My daughters are as different as can be, one an engineer and one a musician. Both are strong young women with feminist sensibilities. They aren't into romance novels, but like millions of other intelligent young adults, they devoured the Harry Potter books. Was the Twilight series like Harry Potter? Was it like our family favorites, *The Hobbit* and Lord of the Rings?

Finally I couldn't take it any more. Early one morning while everyone else slept in, I snuck off with *Twilight* and a pot of coffee. Hours later I emerged, enlightened. I now understood why my daughter had said I would want to read it. Tucked into the pages of these thick, vampiric novels were most of the basic questions of systematic theology; all the issues involved in evangelism in postmodern culture; and many dynamics involving gender, power, and the church. I am a theologian. I teach evangelism. I love great stories. I was hooked.

What Is Twilight?

By the time I finished the last volume, I could hardly wait to prepare a lecture on the gospel according to *Twilight*. Heck, I could do a whole series of lectures! No wonder girls everywhere adore this story—it engages all the emotional, physical, and spiritual awakenings that are common to young women. Stephenie Meyer gets it. Bella is, in so many ways, Everygirl.

The story goes like this: Edward Cullen and his family are "vegetarian" vampires who practice self-control (drinking animal blood rather than human) out of a sense of obligation to the greater good of the world. Although he appears to be about seventeen, Edward is actually decades older, his countenance having been frozen in time when he was made a vampire in 1918. Edward's adoptive vampire father, Carlisle, is a physician in the small town of Forks, Washington. When Isabella ("Bella") Swan, the seventeen-year-old daughter of the divorced sheriff of Forks, comes to live with her father, she meets the Cullen family. Soon Edward and Bella fall in love. Through many harrowing adventures, Bella, Edward, and other characters wrestle with their deepest questions about God, the meaning of life, and the redeeming power of love. (Spoiler alert: if you read beyond this page you're going to get some of the most exciting plot twists from the books.)

Like J. K. Rowling, author of the Harry Potter series, Stephenie Meyer was a new, unknown author when she attempted to publish her unusual vampire romance. After rejections from fourteen publishers (who are now likely kicking themselves), her manuscript for *Twilight* was accepted by Little, Brown, and Company. Four years later the saga had sold over 53 million copies worldwide, with translation rights sold in forty-three countries; to date over a hundred million copies of the series have been sold. The final volume, *Breaking Dawn*, broke publishing records when it sold 1.3 million copies the first day it was released in 2008.[1] The first three Twilight movies grossed $1.75 billion in global box office receipts.[2]

Stephenie Meyer is a Mormon, a fact that amazes many commentators who like to refer to her as "a Mormon housewife." Neither Mormons nor housewives should be capable of publishing wonders, it would seem. But Meyer's theological formation and her work as a mother and homemaker are part of the reason she captures so brilliantly the imaginations of girls everywhere. Because she has so much influence with young women, I wanted to explore in depth just what is going on theologically in these books. Is the gospel according to Twilight good news for girls and women? Is it consistent with Christian faith?

The Gospel according to Twilight

As the day drew near for me to present my first lecture on the gospel according to *Twilight*, I gathered a few extra goodies to help. A short film segment would be important since I imagined students probably had not read the book. We would watch the famed "meadow scene," a watershed romantic moment in the book and the film. At the grocery store check-out line I found heart-shaped candies that said, "I Heart Edward" and "Bite Me." A bowl of juicy apples? Definitely.

I began class by asking how many people had read *Twilight*. The women looked around sheepishly, slowly raising their hands. I had seminary students whose book bags were filled with Augustine, Wesley, Tillich, and *Twilight*. I realized I'd been wrong in thinking that my students wouldn't already be familiar with the series—some of them were already diehard fans or were surrounded by others who were. One of the men admitted his daughters were crazy about the series. A youth pastor nodded. The girls in his youth group were fanatical, too, he reported. They told him, "Edward is hot," or "I'm on Team Jacob."

There wouldn't be time in one class to cover all the themes of the series, so I gave a brief overview, then narrowed the focus to the Adam and Eve subtext in the love story between Edward and Bella. The creation and fall narratives of Genesis are found everywhere in popular culture, something our class had examined the previous week. A woman enticing a man with an apple is one of the most common motifs. We had seen this image in fine art, television programs, and advertisements for everything from plumbing to perfume.

As we watched the meadow scene, I noticed how engrossed the students were in the story. When Edward told Bella she was his own brand of heroin, the class roared with laughter. Someone shouted, "Great pick up line!" A lively discussion followed as we looked at images of gender, power, and seduction in *Twilight* that deliberately play on the Genesis narrative.

I highlighted the good news and bad news of this part of the story, especially for women. The undisputable good news is that life is sacred for Bella, for the vampires who choose not to drink her blood, and for several other characters. This is true whether one reads the story through Catholic, Orthodox, Protestant, or Mormon lenses.

Then things get tricky. When read through a traditional, patriarchal Christian lens, which is true for a vast number of readers, Bella and Edward look just like Adam and Eve in misogynist readings of Genesis. The beautiful and seductive Eve/Bella entices a perfect but vulnerable Adam/Edward with forbidden fruit—in this case, her own body and blood. Viewed in this way, *Twilight* becomes indistinguishable from many other pop culture examples such as plumbing ads.

The morally superior Adam/Edward resists her for a long time but finally caves. Who can blame him? He may be a vampire, but he is a man. But first they must get married, even though Bella, eighteen by this point in the saga, doesn't want to. *Eighteen!*

What century is this? In fact, elements of the relationship between Edward and Bella make the hair stand up on feminist Christian necks, especially when you add in the bit where Bella scarcely survives the violence of her wedding night. Though broken and bruised the next morning, she begs for more. This part of the story is terrible news for girls and women—unless you read it through another lens, such as Stephenie Meyer's. The Eve story has an entirely different meaning in LDS theology, with Eve as a moral heroine who sacrifices her life so that others can live—a theme we'll explore in more detail in chapter 4.

What is going on here? Is Bella a Christ figure, offering her body and blood for others' salvation? Or is she a sex-hungry temptress who's willing to go to hell if she can just have her guy? Is Bella fallen or redemptive or both?

The Genesis subtext can be read in several ways, all quite different—which is exactly why youth pastors, parents, and readers themselves need to pay attention. Like Harry Potter, the Twilight series has the potential to help readers bend toward the Light, especially if they are helped to think theologically about what they are reading. What is the meaning of salvation? Are we saved by being good and doing good works, or is salvation about grace? Is heaven only in the hereafter, or do we begin to live in heaven while we're still on earth? What about hell? Is it real, is it a place, and if so, who goes there?

And speaking of religion, even though Edward insists that they get married for moral reasons and out of concern for Bella's soul, Bella doesn't care about God or heaven. Edward is her heaven. That's what she tells Carlisle, who strongly believes in God. The vampires are far more religious than the humans in this story. They are, as indicated by the playful title of Beth Felker Jones's book *Touched by a Vampire,* almost angelic. The vampires believe God exists, and they make moral choices based partly on their hope for a good reward in eternity. While the characters do not claim to be religious and in many ways are critical of organized religion, they are spiritual, and they think and talk about theological themes.

For that reason evangelism is also at the heart of the saga. In many ways the Twilight saga gives voice to the questions and frustrations of millions of "spiritual but not religious" young adults today. Anyone who cares about evangelism should take note. Within these pages we find wonderful social critiques, especially in regard to racial reconciliation, religious exclusivism, and political and religious oppression. While most of the applause for Twilight from interested religious folk has been directed toward the sexual abstinence theme (and Lord knows we need help in this department), I think the strongest Christian messages in the story have to do with justice and peace. The books also delve into the role of desire in spirituality. Despite significant problems with gender and abuse themes, which we will discuss in part 1 of this book, the Twilight narrative is a captivating story in which theology plays an important role.

I Listened to Every Word

About a month after my class on the gospel according to *Twilight* I had the privilege of preaching at our seminary chapel service for graduating seniors. While praying about the topic of my sermon, I thought about the central role that desire plays in how we live our lives and whether we are faithful to our call. I wanted to preach a sermon that would help graduates think about desire and vocation. How should I talk about desire, I wondered? Should I use a sermon illustration from Plato about reason, appetite, and will?

Suddenly I remembered the cover for *Twilight* and the vigorous discussion in my class. I would talk about Edward and Bella. A few days later I stood in the pulpit surveying the packed chapel. I noticed the dean and some other faculty close to the front. What would they think of my vampire plans? Scattered throughout the pews were young women, some of them students, some graduates, and some there to celebrate the graduation of a loved one. It was time to begin.

"Vampires don't really have scary fangs," I began. "That is an old wives' tale. According to Edward, who ought to know." Some of the young women snapped to attention. "Edward is a vampire," I continued, "the main squeeze in the huge pop culture phenomenon, Twilight. Edward says that everything about vampires is designed to entice their victims through *desire*. So *real* vampires are beautiful, handsome, athletic, exotic, fragrant, delicious . . . irresistible. What is this force called desire?" I asked. The young women leaned forward, waiting.

I paused, noticing that one of the older people in the audience looked alarmed. Why was the seminary professor preaching about vampires? What kind of school was this? Glancing at the dean I noticed the corners of his mouth hinting at a smile. I continued through the rest of the sermon. Desire for the Lord will take us through thick and thin, I preached. Love will empower us to do things that duty and fear cannot. If our desire for God is cultivated, everything else will follow as it should.

At the close of the service a group of young women rushed up, grinning from ear to ear. "I listened to every word of your sermon," one said. All her friends nodded. "I usually don't like sermons," she added, "but as soon as you mentioned Edward I knew it was going to be great!"

Whether it was great I do not know. What has become very clear to me, however, is the power of popular culture to shape our imaginations and our hearts. A great story, even one about vampires, can open us to the influence of the Holy Spirit in ways that a theological statement cannot.

In this book I offer a critical exploration of the major theological themes found in the Twilight saga.[3] I am reading the texts as a feminist theologian, a pastor, and a lover of good stories. I am also reading as someone who cares deeply about the spiritual formation and well-being of girls and women. While I have taken into account some of the things others are saying about Twilight, and I have surveyed nearly two hundred young women and girls who have read the series, this book is my own set of ruminations. It is my hope that this volume might help youth pastors, campus ministers, students of religion and popular culture, and especially the readers of Twilight to critically engage the gospel the saga presents. Although some aspects of the series ought to alarm all of us, there is much in these hefty novels that is delicious.

Part One

An Eclipse of Women

Family, Sex, Gender, and Power in Twilight

Chapter One

The Good Family

Every great story lives in a narrative universe with its own internal logic. Readers quickly come to recognize the logic of the story world. In Tolkien's Middle-earth, for example, hobbits are comfort-loving creatures of small stature who fear going on adventures with wizards. Because of this "fact" about hobbits, readers are increasingly captivated by the courage of Frodo and Sam, who risk comfort and safety in order to resist evil. A coherent narrative universe is one of the ways we enter and are "caught up" in the story.

In the Twilight series, the narrative universe is all about family: family values, the creation of families, broken families, longing for family. The family is the water in which all the Twilight characters swim, whether human, vampire, or wolf. Messages about the importance of family in Twilight are in some ways exemplary from a Christian point of view. Stable, healthy families, after all, are the basic building blocks for strong communities. On the other hand, what constitutes a "good" family in the gospel according to Twilight? Who are they? What do they do that makes them "good"? And is the ideal family in this story compatible with the good family according to Jesus? Because family is the basic element of the narrative universe in Twilight, we will begin there with our theological investigation.

The Exemplary Family

In one of the many ironies of Twilight, the exemplary good family is not human. The parents, Carlisle and Esme Cullen, and their children—Edward, Rosalie, Emmett, Jasper, and Alice—are vampires. Though a family, none of them is "blood kin," at least not in the traditional sense of that term. The whole family was created the vampire way, through biting and venom, a terrifying and agonizing experience. The Cullens' history together began when Carlisle, who had been lonely for centuries, decided to create a family for himself (*Twilight*, 341). (More about his transformation into a vampire in chapter 5, on salvation.)

Because he had disciplined himself to withstand the scent of human blood, choosing to feed on animal blood instead, Carlisle was able over a long period of time to become a physician. It was his way of offering himself as an agent of healing instead of death in the world, though doing so was contrary to his vampire nature. Edward's birth mother, before succumbing to influenza in 1918, sensed that her doctor, Carlisle, had supernatural powers. With her last breath she made him promise to save Edward, also at death's door. Carlisle did so, after a fashion: he gave Edward the gift of immortality.

Thus Carlisle became Edward's father, healer, and "savior," through transforming him into a vampire. A man of principle, Carlisle's pattern through the decades was only to "change" those unfortunates who were about to die anyway. Esme, who became Carlisle's wife, was on the point of death from suicide when Carlisle changed her. She had thrown herself off a cliff after losing her unborn child and running away from an abusive marriage. Rosalie, Edward's adoptive sister, was the victim of a brutal sexual assault at the hands of several men, including her drunken fiancé.[1] Emmett, who is married to Rosalie, had been mauled by a bear before Rosalie brought him to Carlisle, who changed him.

Other family members were not Carlisle's creations. Alice was adopted into the Cullen family after she became a vampire. She is married to Jasper, who was also already a vampire before coming into the family. Jasper and Emmett, who are in the family through marriage, are as much a part of the Cullen clan as the adopted children. All of them follow Carlisle's lead, drinking animal instead of human blood and fitting in as much as possible with ordinary human society. The "vegetarian" diet is hardest for Jasper, whose life prior to the Cullen family had been dark indeed.

All of this adds up to a family in which every member is a survivor of unbelievable violence, yet they have chosen to live peaceably in the world. They have decided not to pass their history of violence on to others. Carlisle's example and leadership are critical in the formation of his family's ethos. He is the linchpin of virtue. The Good Family is good primarily because it has a loving father at the helm. (He's also incredibly handsome.)

In addition to a strong, responsible, emotionally present father, the Cullen family has a nurturing mother. Like all the Cullens, Esme was changed as a young adult, so she is frozen at age twenty-six in terms of her appearance. Slender, beautiful, and yet "soft" looking, Esme's predominant feature is her selfless capacity to love others. Gentle and hospitable to a fault, Esme anticipates the needs of everyone around her. The first time Bella comes to the Cullen house, Esme prepares for her a meal of Italian food, though human food is repulsive to vampires. She doesn't want Bella to be hungry. Esme works hard to make sure their home is welcoming and beautiful, including keeping vases of fresh-cut flowers scattered about at all times. Her hobby is the restoration of historic buildings. When Edward and Bella get married, Esme restores an old cottage in the woods to serve as their first home. She is the quintessential domestic mother, tender and sweet, who clearly looks to Carlisle as the head of the home.

All of the Cullen children are highly educated, partly because they have so much time on their undead hands. Once they finish high school and college, in order not to blow their cover by remaining eternally young while their neighbors age, they move to another city. There they repeat the cycle. Carlisle is always able to get work in a local hospital, and the "children" enroll in school once again. (This explains why Edward is so knowledgeable about the phases of mitosis when he is Bella's lab partner.) Prior to coming to Forks, Washington, the setting for the Twilight saga, the Cullens lived in Denali, Alaska.

Thanks to Carlisle's ample income and Alice's ability to forecast what is happening on the stock market, the family is rich. Their massive garage is loaded with luxury automobiles, something for everyone's taste. Their spectacular home is secluded in the forest, with entire walls made of glass. Rather than a safe room, they have an impenetrable, opaque shield that can be raised outside the glass walls if needed, protecting the entire house from would-be intruders. Tasteful furnishings and artwork create an environment of elegance and comfort. No cellars, coffins, or cobwebs for these vampires; their house is filled with warmth and light.

This is an ideal American family with perfect looks, perfect clothes, a perfect house, perfect cars, perfect education, perfect parents, perfect children, and a perfect financial portfolio. They are living the American Dream.

To stress the American part, the Cullens' favorite family activity is baseball. (Because of the thunderous noise made when they hit the ball with their supernatural strength, they must go into a secluded meadow during a thunderstorm to play; otherwise the humans in Forks would hear them.) In baseball as in everything else, Carlisle is in charge. When a group of roving vampires discovers the Cullens in the meadow playing ball, they negotiate with Carlisle, the patriarch, about joining the game. This is a perfect family that James Dobson (the founder of Focus on the Family)[2] would love, one in which father knows best, mother is "soft" and serves, and all the children obey—even after they are married.

The Cullens are also a great example of the perfect LDS family.[3] (LDS stands for Latter-day Saint, or Mormon, like Stephenie Meyer.) Ideal LDS families are patriarchal, refrain from consuming caffeine and alcohol, observe family time on Monday nights, and are kind to their neighbors. In the Cullen family, Carlisle is the benevolent but patriarchal leader. The family is "vegetarian," refraining from blood instead of caffeine or drugs, and they play baseball, hunt, and do other activities together. Marriage and family commitments are supreme because in LDS theology marriages and families are forever, with devout couples moving from this mortal life into the Celestial Kingdom (the highest level of heaven) where they procreate into infinity.[4] As we will see in subsequent chapters, vampires in Twilight mate for life; in the case of the Cullens, we have a family that can live into eternity.

In her book *Touched by a Vampire*, evangelical Christian writer Beth Felker Jones makes a clear distinction between Christian messages and Mormon messages in Twilight, a division that is offensive to Latter-day Saints, who consider themselves Christian.[5] The two moral universes are not the same, Jones writes, and discerning Christian readers should note where there are significant differences, using the Bible as a guide for reflection. Some of her critique of Twilight has to do with Meyer's LDS idealization of family life, which she sees as deviating from the Bible's message about God's love shining through weak, flawed humans, including less-than-perfect families.[6] Whether one reads Twilight through Protestant, Catholic, Orthodox, or LDS lenses, it is clear that the Cullens are meant to be seen as the exemplary Good Family.

The Damaged Family

Ironically, Bella's father Charlie Swan, who in general dislikes and distrusts Edward Cullen, raves about what a great family the Cullens are. They stick together, play together, and have mature parents, he says (Twilight, 36–37). Although Charlie doesn't know it, the family that preys together stays together.

The perfection of the good Cullen family stands in stark contrast to the flawed Swans, whose failed marriage and family life is the fault of Renee, Bella's stuck-in-emotional-adolescence mother. Bella's parents are not bad people, but they are divorced, the only divorced parents in the book. In the narrative universe of Twilight, divorce means defective.

From early childhood Bella has been her mother's caretaker. Bella was "born middle-aged," far more responsible and aware than her flighty mother (Twilight, 106). Throughout her life Bella has known her mother as needy, immature, undisciplined, and sometimes selfish. Renee walked out on Charlie when Bella was an infant because Renee didn't want to be trapped in the small town of Forks.

Bella has spent most of her childhood cooking, cleaning, and maintaining stability in her home with her mother. She has rarely visited her father, whom she calls Charlie. When Renee begins dating during Bella's adolescence, it is Bella who gives her mother "the talk" about sexual responsibility (*Eclipse*, 67). Bella's descriptions of her mother are condescending and at times bordering on contempt. (This is one of several characterizations in the novels that is smoothed over or completely changed in the movies.) Bella disapproves of Renee's new husband, who "allows" Renee to engage in dangerous activities such as skydiving. But like a mother sighing over her daughter's loser boyfriend, Bella concludes that she really has to let her mother make her own choices even when those choices are wrong (*Eclipse*, 45).

Renee's dysfunction is comprehensive. On the trivial side, she is unable to grow flowers around her mailbox because she can't figure out how to water and tend them. The inability to nurture, however, goes far beyond flowers. When Renee marries a second-rate baseball player named Phil and moves to Florida to be with him, she does so with no thought for disrupting Bella's junior year in high school. In essence she emotionally abandons Bella, causing Bella to move to Forks to live with her dad.

The first e-mail Bella receives from her mother on arriving in Forks is a childish plea for Bella to help her find her pink blouse, which she has misplaced. She is packing to go off with Phil and can't find her own clothes (*Twilight*, 33). When Bella is in the hospital recovering from a near-fatal vampire attack, she remarks that her mother's concern for her recovery is the first time she has experienced anything like parental authority from Renee since she was eight years old (*Twilight*, 468). Incredibly, Renee chooses to miss Bella's graduation from high school because Phil breaks his leg and Renee thinks she is the only one on earth who can take care of him (*Eclipse*, 314). Renee, who is clueless about how to care for her own daughter, is utterly enmeshed with her young new husband.

Renee is not the only helpless parent in this story. Charlie, who has lived alone ever since Renee walked out on him, is unable to cook or clean for himself. When Bella arrives in Forks, she quickly discovers that Charlie needs the same kind of domestic caretaking that she has provided for Renee most of her life. At one point Bella catches him trying to microwave a jar of spaghetti sauce with the lid on. He is unable even to boil pasta (*Twilight*, 31; *Eclipse*, 5).

Bella does the grocery shopping, cleans the house, and assumes all the cooking, and Charlie is only too happy to agree to this arrangement. When Charlie comes in from work, he expects her to get his supper as if he were the child and she were the parent (*Twilight*, 295). Despite Charlie's ineptitude at home, however, he somehow manages to be a responsible sheriff. The rest of Charlie's life consists of going fishing with friends and watching endless hours of ESPN. Though he loves Bella, he is awkward at expressing any feelings other than mumbled thanks for her meals or occasional bursts of irritation or worry.

When Charlie provides Bella with snow tires for her truck, she is stunned by his kindness because, as already noted, she is not used to a parent taking care of her (*Twilight*, 55). The one thing Bella is especially grateful for with Charlie is that he is as uncomfortable with emotional exchanges and conversation as she is. They quietly live together in the same house, but with very little communication beyond small talk.

Divorce has not only left her parents dysfunctional and underdeveloped; it has dehumanized Bella, who has never been close to anyone except for her caretaking role with her mother (*Twilight*, 10–11). She discovers with bitter humor after coming to Forks that when she finally does develop true friendships for the first time in her life, it is with vampires and werewolves (*New Moon*, 294)! Bella, who is filled with self-loathing and sees herself as cursed with bad luck, is unable to be intimate in a normal way with other humans, whether they are parents, friends, or boyfriends. Bella's lifelong alienation stems in large part from her parents' divorce, which has turned both parents into dysfunctional, needy adults who have neither the time nor the wisdom to provide Bella with the nurture and freedom she needed to be a child.

There are other consequences, too. Because of her parents' divorce, especially Renee's warnings against marrying too young, Bella is appalled when Edward proposes to her. She doesn't see the point of marriage and thinks that she and Edward should be sexually intimate without it. Her aversion to marriage has nothing to do with her commitment to Edward. It is all about her parents' failed marriage (*New Moon*, 540–41). In this way the divorce has also been demoralizing for Bella.

Bella's longing to become a vampire is as much about wanting to belong to the ideal Cullen family as it is about her love for Edward. When the Cullens disappear after an incident in *New Moon* in which a blood-crazed Jasper tries to attack Bella, she is plunged into a long, terrible grief. Her depression is beyond telling, not only because she loses Edward but because she loses her dream of belonging in a real family (*New Moon*, 398, 401). The Cullens have successfully evangelized her to their Good Family through their love, protection, compassion, humor, playfulness, and inclusion. Then suddenly, they vanish. Though they do this for Bella's protection as well as for their own safety and that of the people of Forks, their disappearance is more than Bella can bear. Her love for Edward cannot be extracted from her love for his family.

Toward the end of the last novel, *Breaking Dawn,* a vampire named Garrett makes a defiant speech to the Volturi (the elite group of vampires who rule the undead world) about the powerful virtue he has witnessed in the Cullen family. He emphasizes that unlike other small groups of vampires around the world, the Cullens are a *family*, not a coven. He claims that their power of self-denial and self-control is more potent than the power of fear and coercion used by the Volturi. Garrett marvels at the Cullens' peaceful way of life, which demonstrates the ultimate power of love. He begins to think that there are things more important than self-gratification, an idea that the Cullens model for others (*Breaking Dawn*, 717).

By the end of the story the Cullens' love has healed family-of-origin wounds not only in Bella but also in Nehuel, a half human/half vampire who killed his own mother. He comes to see Bella and Edward as the parents he never had and begins to live according to the ways of the Good Family (*Breaking Dawn*, 750–51). Bella, Edward, and Renesmee, their own half-human/half-vampire daughter, morph into a "super family." Through their incarnation of racial reconciliation and their shielding of many humans and innocent vampires from Volturi injustice, they are able to resist evil and become conduits of grace. Grounded in the Cullen family through marriage and pregnancy, Bella finally comes to believe that a mysterious goodness is at work in the world, and that there is a larger story unfolding that has real meaning. She names the new awareness "faith" (*Breaking Dawn*, 190). Thus Bella awakens to the spiritual life through her immersion in the Good Family.

A Closer Look at Family Values

What implicit messages does Twilight communicate about family, marriage, and singleness? How do these messages square with the gospel according to Jesus? The idea of a nonhuman family as the archetype for the Good Family is surprisingly consistent with Jesus' prophetic stories. He often uses outsiders and despised or rejected "others" as exemplars in narratives that call God's people back to right living. For example, when Jesus wants to demonstrate what it means to love our neighbors, he tells the story of the Good Samaritan (Luke 10:30–37). In this parable a despised outsider, a Samaritan, is the one who exemplifies virtue. The insiders— religious leaders—are morally defective. The story of the Good Samaritan is especially poignant because the character who exemplifies virtue is racially and religiously stigmatized by Jesus' listeners. Samaritans, whose heritage was half-Jewish and half-Gentile, were hated by Jews for being racially and religiously mixed.

By choosing vampires to model what real family life is supposed to be while presenting human families as broken and weak, Stephenie Meyer offers a sharp critique of human family life today. Plagued with divorce, immaturity, absentee parents, and worse, families—including Christians—have much to learn from the Cullens. Would that more human families had two parents who loved each other and their children, children who respected their parents, priorities that included playing together and protecting each other, and a mission—passing on to the world at large the healing and protective energy of their family. One can scarcely think of a more striking "other" to use as an archetype for a healthy family than a pack of blood-sucking and possibly damned souls. This is a prophetic move of which Jesus would likely approve.

Another element to the Good Family that is profoundly rooted in the gospel of Jesus is that the Cullens are all survivors of sin and violence, yet they have chosen the way of peace. Though their instinct is to deceive and prey on humans, the Cullens choose a path of self-denial, drinking animal blood instead of human. They have created a lifestyle and habitat that is most conducive to safety—not just for themselves but also for the humans around them. Not only do they avoid doing the evil that is natural for them, they choose to create a loving family and use their family strength to do good, to be a source of life for the human community. Carlisle's work as a physician is especially notable here.

So in this way the Cullen family is symbolic of a foundational teaching of Jesus: divine love enables people to avoid evil and to do what is good. Jesus teaches that the love of God is stronger than normal survival instincts, even the most basic appetite for food. When Jesus went to the desert for a season of temptation, Satan tested him through elemental human needs (Luke 4:1–13). The temptations centered not on sinful desires or needs, since the desires for food and protection from harm are not sinful, but on inappropriate timing or methods for meeting those needs. Jesus faced temptations around hunger (turning the stones to bread), worship and life orientation (Satan shows Jesus the kingdoms of the world), and his own identity ("If you are the Son of God . . ."). The temptations had to do with meeting these needs in the wrong way or at the wrong time. In all of these basic human needs Jesus chose to love and honor God rather than serve himself. By relying on God's power, especially manifested through Scripture, Jesus had the power to endure temptation involving the most elemental human drives. (It is the self-denial Christians remember when we celebrate Lent in some traditions.)

The third way the Cullens as the Good Family are consistent with the gospel of Jesus is that they are a family not by virtue of birth but by choice. They are in fact unrelated persons who have created a strong family community that is bound together by a spirituality of love. They are in this way archetypal of a healthy faith community, a microcongregation.

Despite American Christians' emphasis on the nuclear family, when Jesus focuses on the family in the Gospels he is talking about the family of God. According to Mark 3:20–35, at one point early in his ministry, Jesus' mother and brothers come looking for him, convinced that he has lost his mind. They want to take him home to protect him from himself, and possibly to protect themselves from further public embarrassment. Jesus looks around at the crowd that has gathered and says, "'Whoever does the will of God is my brother and sister and mother'" (Mark 3:35).

At another time while he is teaching, a woman cries out from the crowd, "'Blessed is the womb that bore you and the breasts that nursed you!'" (Luke 11:27). She is paying Jesus a traditional type of compliment by saying how blessed Jesus' mother (and by extension, family of origin) must be to have Jesus in the family. How surprised she must be to hear Jesus' response! His answer to the woman is not meant to disrespect his mother, Mary, or his family of origin but to reinforce the larger importance of the family of God: "'Blessed rather are those who hear the word of God and obey it!'" (Luke 11:28). Jesus has a different view of family. When he focuses on the family, it is the family of God.

In these three ways, then, the Cullens exemplify the family values of Jesus in the Gospels. Although they are by nature monsters in the eyes of humans, they illustrate a loving family more than the humans do. They've transcended their own histories as victims of violence and forged a life of peace and service to the world. The Cullens are a Good Family not by virtue of natural birth but because they have become an intentional community of love. They are a *family*, as Garrett stresses, not a *coven*.

But there is another side to the Good Family, two ways in which the Cullens are anything but a good family according to the gospel of Jesus. First, their existence in the human community is a deception. Their whole way of life is based on a skillfully woven set of lies. As Bella prepares for her "conversion" to a vampire, she ponders the importance of keeping the Cullen family's secrets. She knows that she cannot ever tell anyone outside the family what the family really is. To do so would threaten the existence of not just

the Cullens but vampires everywhere (*Breaking Dawn*, 32–33).
She would blow their cover. Although such secrecy makes sense
in the context of the story, it presents a deep problem in the gospel
according to Twilight. In the real world of readers, part of life in
shame-based, alcoholic and/or abusive families includes the strict
keeping of family secrets. Shame, guilt, fear, and threats are used
to keep family members in the system so that the family's true
condition is hidden from outsiders. Healing requires breaking the
code of silence and telling the truth. Indeed it is a common maxim
for survivors of abuse that "the healing is in the telling." Deception
as a way of life and its related rule of keeping family secrets is a
problem in this Good Family.

The second and equally pernicious way that the Cullens diverge
from Jesus' gospel is that they are utterly materialistic with their
money. What do they do with all their wealth? How do they
spend the millions of dollars they obtain from their clairvoyantly
acquired investments? Do they use it to alleviate poverty, to provide clean water and food for the 27,000 children in the world who
die every day from preventable causes, or to address the epidemic
of HIV/AIDS in Africa? Heck, do they even use it to preserve
wilderness lands so that their prey will have somewhere to live a
hundred years from now? No.

Instead the Cullens shop, shop, shop, and only at the most
expensive stores. They have fancy silver cell phones and special
black credit cards. Alice makes sure they rarely wear the same
designer garment twice. Their numerous luxury cars are fashion accessories for their various outings. On her engagement to
Edward, Bella receives a Mercedes Guardian (based on the Mercedes S600 Guard), a car used to protect heads of state and drug
lords from assassination. Edward wants to make sure she survives
until the wedding, after which she will become a vampire and not
require special protection. Esme owns an entire island in South
America, just a little getaway for now and then. The Cullens are
rolling in money, yet it appears they spend every dime on themselves. This is not the value system of the Good Family according
to Jesus.

D *is for Defective*

What about the flawed family in this story? Is the portrait of divorce as a situation that produces families that are defective, dehumanized, and demoralized a message that is true? Is this a theme that Christian readers should unthinkingly internalize? Does it reflect the spiritual commitments of Jesus?

According to some Christian traditions, the answer is yes to all of the above. The prohibition against divorce continues to be strong in many denominations, so if a person gets divorced, regardless of the reason, he or she is permanently banned from leadership positions in the church and in some cases cannot take communion. In other words, the divorced are permanently defective. These prohibitions against divorce are mostly based on interpretations of the biblical texts that speak about divorce, especially Malachi 2:16 in the Old Testament and Jesus' teachings in the New Testament.

At first glance it seems that, indeed, divorce is always a dysfunctional choice that is harmful to all concerned, or it wouldn't be presented so restrictively in the Bible. However, a closer look at the contexts of the Scriptures about divorce presents a more nuanced understanding, one that bears important light as we consider the portrait of divorced people in Twilight.

In the Bible there are three circumstances under which divorce may be a tragic but sometimes necessary event. These are the breaking of the marriage covenant through various forms of violence, through sexual infidelity, or through abandonment by an unbelieving spouse. In all three of these situations one of the marriage partners sins against the other through covenant-breaking acts. While it is true that there is always a dynamic involving both marriage partners when there is a divorce, it is unconscionable to blame and punish those who have been sinned against by an abusive, unfaithful, or abandoning spouse.

The implicit message of Twilight—that divorce creates families (and parents) that are defective, dehumanized, and demoralized—simply fails to take into account the many reasons that people get divorced. It presents a flat, negative, and unfair picture of the family that has endured the pain of divorce, and it does not recognize the tremendous courage required for victims of violence, infidelity, or abandonment to say no to being sinned against and to move forward with their lives into healing. There are no relationships that are more defective, dehumanizing or demoralizing than marriages subjected to violence, infidelity, and abandonment. Divorce also does not automatically create incompetent parents who reverse roles with their children, as Twilight seems to suggest. Sometimes it is the first step toward becoming a more loving and responsible parent. Even in the LDS community, with its intense commitment to marriage and family, it is possible under some circumstances to have an eternal marriage "cancelled," something akin to the Catholic process of annulment.[7]

The good news of Jesus is that no matter how broken people may be through divorce, the love of God is able to heal their wounds and make all things new. Divorce is not an unforgivable sin. On the contrary, divorce is sometimes necessary in order to break generational sins of abuse and dysfunction. A divorced family, in other words, can be a "good" family.

The caricature of Charlie and Renee as inept, bumbling, immature, and self-absorbed divorced parents would be forgivable in this story if there were other divorced parents who were healthy and responsible. But because they are the *only* divorced parents, their pervasive dysfunction provides a judgmental, unfair subtext to young readers about the defectiveness of divorced people, one that conflicts with the gracious, healing message of Jesus Christ.

The role reversal of parents and child in the Swan family is more typical in the real world in shame-based families where one or both parents are addicted to alcohol, drugs, or something else. Many adult children of alcoholics reading the Twilight books, for example, can readily identify with Bella's hyperresponsibility for all the domestic chores and her care-taking role with her parents. Though Renee's behavior would be more typical of a mom with a drinking problem, in Twilight almost no one uses or talks about alcohol. Edward makes a metaphoric reference to wine once. The thugs who threaten to harm Bella are outside a bar. That is the closest the book comes to mentioning booze. They may not even drink coffee in Forks. Blood, gore, and mayhem in Twilight? Yes. Mood-altering substances? Absolutely not. Our author is a Mormon.

The narrative universe of family in the Twilight series carries many positive and life-giving messages that are consistent with a Christian message. In particular, the Good Family models the kinds of spirituality and intentional community that are healing for those within and beyond the immediate family. Meyer's story rightly critiques families in which parents and children reverse roles, robbing children of a normal childhood and of the adult supervision they need in order to grow up healthy and whole. At the same time, some of the assumptions about marriage, the Good Family, and divorce are more reflective of consumeristic cultural values and judgmental church practices than of the gospel according to Jesus. In the next chapter we will move from our reflection on families in Twilight to the narrative theme of couples, the basic building block for the family.

Chapter Two

I'm Only Half of Me
The Dread of Being Single in Twilight

*I*n Twilight, as we've seen, the basic unit of the Good Family is a man and woman paired for eternity. At the heart of the narrative universe of family life is the expectation that all "normal" people are with partners. In the world of Twilight no one is complete without a mate. Absolutely every person, vampire, or wolf is but half a being until she or he is in a relationship. No wonder Charlie doesn't know how to boil spaghetti or laugh. He's been *alone*! For *years*!

First there are the high school students. Within an hour of Bella's arrival at Forks High, boys throw themselves at her. Because she is depressed and filled with self-consciousness about what she regards as her awkward existence and the misery of adolescent life, she is not flattered by their attention. Instead, she wants invisibility. Before long, though, Bella meets Edward, and the fireworks begin. Throughout the books the high school students—Angela, Eric, Jessica, Mike, and others—pair off. Unlike the real world of readers, in Forks no one wants to go to the prom just with a group of friends. This is because every single person has to have a date. Nearly all the conversations of the human high school students rotate around romance and upcoming dates.

Things are no different in the vampire world. Carlisle and Esme and Rosalie and Emmett are soul mates. Alice and Jasper are each other's other half (*Eclipse*, 50). Even James and Victoria, the baddies, are bound for the duration of their immortal lives.[1] If someone or something kills a mated vampire, the surviving mate will not stop until he or she destroys the perpetrator. This is why Victoria is determined to kill Bella; she wants to punish Edward, who terminated James, who tried to kill Bella.

All this focus on couples is not surprising in a romance novel about high school students; we expect drama over who's going with whom to the prom. We would be disappointed if there were not mean girls, parties, and a beach. But the incessant pairing of virtually *everyone* introduces plot material that is beyond weird.

Imprints

The werewolves, who we learn in *Breaking Dawn* are technically shape-shifters, are members of the Quileute tribe. Due to a genetic predisposition to produce new generations of sturdy werewolves, an irresistible attraction called "imprinting" causes male Quileutes with the werewolf chromosome to bond for life with mysteriously selected females. One day a Quileute boy feels nothing for a particular girl; the next day imprinting kicks in and voilà, he adores her for the rest of his life. She might be lovely, homely, boring, shrill, kind, or indifferent. It matters not. She has become the love of his life. He will die before he lets anything harm her. In the books, she always agrees to the imprinted pairing. Always. Even though the imprint happens to him, not her. His adoration eventually becomes irresistible.

Jacob describes the sensation of imprinting as a growing heat. It is as if dawn is breaking forth within his soul. Everything within the boy is undone in wonder and adoration as he discovers that his mate is now the center of his existence. The word "love" is too weak to describe what he feels. All the other loves he has experienced in life, all other goodness and joy, are now filtered through the one central love, his mate. She has become his anchor, his sun, his reason for being. She is now the defining point, the interpretive key to all existence. In short, he worships her (*Breaking Dawn*, 359–60).

This is the kind of adoration and unconditional love that young women long to receive. Who wouldn't want to be cherished in this way? But there is a dark side to the brilliance of being worshiped. As anyone who has survived stalking will tell you, it is frightening to be the object of another's obsession. The one who is loved loses her freedom as she is watched, followed, and controlled. The underbelly of this kind of love is violence.

As we've seen, the female recipient of the male imprint has virtually no freedom of choice in her relationships. That freedom is taken away by the male. He waits on her hand and foot and makes her the center of his universe. If he imprints on her when she is a baby, she grows up indoctrinated to the expectation that she will marry him. She is socialized to accept his adoration whether she initially wants it or not or whether she is old enough to understand what is happening, as in the case of Quil (a teenager) and Claire (age two) (*Eclipse*, 176). The female does not experience the sudden imprint emotionally or spiritually in the way the male does. She is the passive recipient of the male's imprint on her. The power of the male over the female is inherent in the process of imprinting.

The loss of freedom for the male is also a problem, because the male cannot exercise choice over his own instincts to mate. He must obey the mysterious urge to imprint. Neither the male nor the female are complete as individuals; they are only half selves until they bond through imprinting. The inevitability of imprinting and its consequences as well as the "half self" message should alarm every Christian reader. As Eric Jepson notes, this element of the story is inconsistent with Meyer's Mormon beliefs, in that "agency," or the complete freedom to make moral and other choices, conflicts with the notion of imprinting.[2]

But the inevitability factor is only the beginning of the dark side. It is not unusual for a male to imprint on a child, who is then prepared by her much older partner to receive his sexual advances once she is of age. A sexually mature Quileute can imprint on a female of any age, including a newborn. Jacob defends Quil's imprinting on the toddler Claire, chastising Bella for being "judgmental" about this way of life.[3] Not only does Jacob go on to imprint on Renesmee at birth, but while she is a toddler he gives her the equivalent of a promise ring. Although he has to wait until she is sexually mature to have her, it is all but inevitable that he *will* have her.

This is the way pedophiles operate. Like a Quileute imprinting on a child, pedophiles carefully groom their victims. The word *pedophile* means one who loves children, and many pedophiles believe that there is a mutual attraction between themselves and the children they target. Pedophilia is almost impossible to treat with any success, partly because of the depth to which many pedophiles believe their own altered reality about children.

No amount of explanations from the author, speaking through Jacob or any other character, can justify this element of the story as anything but appalling. It is outrageously close to what happens to children who are victimized by pedophiles, except that in Twilight the victims live happily ever after with their perpetrators.

There is one more disturbing element to imprinting that needs to be mentioned. The only female werewolf in the story, a girl named Leah, is unable to find a mate. The man/wolf she loves, Sam, has imprinted on a woman named Emily, so Leah suffers the pain of unrequited love. (Emily, by the way, has a severely disfigured face and arm because Sam attacked her while he was out of control one day while phasing into a werewolf. Yet Emily loved and forgave him because he couldn't help it. As we will see, this is one of several examples of a female character in Twilight who is a victim of violence at the hands of her intimate partner.)

Because of Leah's unnatural (for women) "condition" as a werewolf, her sexual identity is ambiguous. Though she is a young woman, the physiological effects of being a werewolf have rendered her prematurely menopausal (*Breaking Dawn*, 317–19). She runs with the guys, hears their thoughts, shares their pack life, and is bitter about her fate. Others don't know how to relate to her androgyny. Leah is cynical and alienated. In the narrative universe of Twilight, she is a misfit (*Breaking Dawn*, 315). Without a mate she cannot be normal or have a fulfilling life. She lives in a nether world between genders.

Leah's marginalized position in the story is in keeping with the LDS vision of the hereafter. Only those who are married can achieve the fullest possible salvation in the Celestial Kingdom, the highest level of the Mormon heaven.[4] Single people do not get to become eternal parents like God. That ultimate blessing is only for those who are married. Whether Meyer intends it or not, Leah personifies a threefold LDS dread of singleness, infertility, and sexual ambiguity.

The real focal point of coupling in this series, though, is the long, slow romance of Edward and Bella. Their relationship is a story of desire, and in the smoldering love that grows between them we encounter everything from the heights of divine attraction to a depraved thirst for blood. First let's examine the bad news about their romance, and then in the next chapter we'll ponder what is good.

A Dangerous Romance Novel

The story of Edward and Bella's love has all the stock features of a romance novel published by Harlequin: a vulnerable, displaced young woman finds herself in an exotic new setting where she meets a mysterious, brooding male. He has exceptionally thick, wavy hair, the kind that falls into his mesmerizing eyes. In the classic romance archetype, the young woman has emerged from a tragedy of some kind and is usually from a social or economic class several notches below the sexy mystery man. She is frugal, considers herself ordinary, and works at some job that doesn't pay well. Because of her multiple layers of vulnerability she catches the attention of the tall, dark, buff stranger, who begins to rescue her from her various (often self-inflicted) dilemmas. The heroine is far more attractive than she knows, exciting the desire of the hero more than she comprehends. Unlike the heroine, the hero is wealthy, powerful, experienced, charismatic, and given to . . . mood swings.

Yes, the stock hero of romance novels is a complicated fellow. His past is hidden in the mists of tragedy and unmet need, and he is tormented with conflicting desires toward the vulnerable heroine. Because he is unwilling to tell her exactly what is going on in his anguished mind, he reacts to her with wild mood swings and mixed messages that leave her wondering if she is crazy. Melancholy one moment, ecstatic the next, he is as likely to fly into a rage as bring his beloved a diamond.

Does this sound just a little worrisome to you? It should. These are also characteristics of abusive men.[5] Just as the practice of imprinting normalizes what is pedophilic in the real world of readers, many aspects of Edward and Bella's relationship normalize abuse in the name of love. This is more than a romance novel. It is a story that is potentially dangerous to young readers who may internalize abuse as an acceptable part of the romance package.

Crazy Making

Let's begin with moods. Survivors of domestic violence and dating violence often speak of their violent partner as a Dr. Jekyll and Mr. Hyde. He has more than one personality, and you never know from one day or one hour to the next, which will manifest. The mood swings and the different "selves" keep the victim of violence off guard and confuse her. When the violent partner is challenged for his previous statements and actions that hurt the victim, he either denies them or has a smooth explanation that is hard to refuse. Often he turns the situation around so that it looks like *he* is the victim. He is a master at this kind of game. Many survivors describe this as "crazy making" because they begin to question their own experience and perceptions, and eventually, their own sanity. The longer survivors endure this kind of Jekyll-and-Hyde behavior, the more isolated and insane they feel. It is one of the ways abusers keep control, and for the abusive partner it is all about control.

Edward's crazy-making behavior begins the moment he meets Bella. On her first day at Forks High School, Bella is assigned a seat next to Edward in Biology. As she sits down she notices that Edward seems hostile, even furious, toward her even though they have never met (*Twilight*, 27). Later on she sees him glaring at her with "piercing, hate-filled eyes," and she is terrified (*Twilight*, 27). He is absent the next couple of days, and when he returns, she experiences her first of many episodes of emotional whiplash. Edward is gracious, friendly, welcoming, and utterly charming. His warmth catches Bella off guard, confusing her. Then accidentally his hand brushes hers, causing him to clench his fists and become avoidant again. Bella begins to feel crazy (*Twilight*, 43–46).

Things intensify when Bella is almost crushed by a van in the icy parking lot at school. Edward, who sees the out-of-control van hurtling toward Bella, uses his super speed to rush over, lift the van away from her with his hand, and shield Bella from injury. He moves so fast behind the cover of the van that other students aren't aware of what he has done. But Bella sees and knows. Later, in the hospital where she has been evaluated for injury, Bella asks Edward how he did it. He denies her reality, points out that she has a concussion, and accuses her of imagining things. He moves from chuckling to cold fury in a matter of syllables, not because of anything Bella says or does that is wrong but because he doesn't want her to know the truth about what he is. Edward becomes enraged, then conciliatory as he begs her to trust him even though he refuses to offer an explanation of how he saved her. Again, he denies her reality and acts as if Bella is mentally unstable. She stares at him, stunned and intimidated by his rage. Bella says that it is like trying to "stare down a destroying angel" (*Twilight*, 54–65). The scene ends with Edward storming off, livid.

This cycle continues to repeat itself in the weeks that follow, with Bella beginning to feel attracted to Edward during his charming moments. She recognizes that she is afraid of him and that his mood swings hurt and confuse her, but she is fascinated by him anyway. During Edward's dark moods he speaks and acts disrespectfully to her. For example, during one of their conversations in which he goes through rapid mood changes, he tells her with inexplicable anger that she is "exceptionally unobservant." In frustration Bella asks if he has multiple personality disorder (*Twilight*, 81–82). She begins to think she cannot trust her own perceptions because she can't tell where she stands with him. Then, when she has just about decided he will never like her, he asks her to sit with him in the cafeteria.

As their relationship progresses to friendship and then dating,

Edward's mercurial behavior escalates. He is obsessed with her but fearful of losing control of himself and the relationship. Bella interprets his dark moods entirely in terms of the pain of his distancing from her rather than his dysfunction (*Twilight*, 365). Although the mood swings frighten, confuse, and disorient her, she stays in the relationship because she has bonded with the part of him that is good and loving. She describes the feeling that is all too common to women who are emotionally and psychologically abused: "It was hard to keep up—his sudden mood changes always left me a step behind, dazed" (*Twilight*, 266).

Even after they are married and on their honeymoon, Bella suffers from Edward's anger. When she becomes pregnant, Edward's response is rage. With cold, harsh movements he packs all their belongings and informs her they are returning to Forks. Bella is frightened. She does not understand why he is so angry (*Breaking Dawn*, 130–31). Readers learn that Edward feels guilty and angry with himself because impregnating Bella has put her life at risk. But what Bella *experiences* is Edward's anger at the pregnancy, including his emotionally and physically distancing himself from her. This distancing is the most painful thing Edward can do to Bella. Many abusive men withhold sex, affection, money, and other basic needs in order to punish and manipulate their partners.

Rage

Physical violence is just one of many ways male abusers control their partners, and the use of force isn't always applied directly to the woman. Sometimes the perpetrator breaks or hurts objects, such as punching holes in the wall, throwing dishes, smashing objects, and so on. Often the breaking of objects is calculated to threaten her so that she knows she could be next. He tears up a book that she loves, or breaks her bicycle, or drop-kicks her cat. In addition to physical violence, he may threaten her verbally with hints about what he might do if he gets angry or doesn't get his way. He may drive recklessly to intimidate her.[6]

Bella experiences many of these forms of violence from Edward. Early in their relationship before they date, Edward begins to control Bella's movements by telling her he wants to drive her when he learns that she wants to go to Seattle. When she resists, he comes up with many reasons why he should drive her and she shouldn't drive herself. He has previously told her in no uncertain terms that he doesn't want to be friends with her. Not surprisingly, Bella asks him why he would want to drive her to Seattle when he already said he doesn't want to be friends. Edward responds with a warning that lets her know she should do what he says, even though he could hurt her. It is safer, more prudent for her to stay away from him, he says, with smoldering eyes. But he has decided that despite endangering her, he is tired of trying to avoid her. He has given in to his desire, and that means he wants to drive her to Seattle. This answer both frightens and thrills Bella. She is excited by the desire that she sees in his eyes. But what kind of danger is he promising? What could go wrong? She caves and allows him to drive, despite all the warning signs for potential violence (*Twilight*, 83–84).

As they go to Seattle, Edward drives like a maniac, a control-and-intimidation tactic common to abusive men. Hurtling at over 100 miles per hour through the forest on winding curves, Edward laughs at Bella's fear. While he jets along through fog and trees, his eyes are off the road and on Bella. It is a fantasy world in which Edward never gets a ticket or wrecks the car; what he does get is more control over Bella.[7]

After they begin dating, Edward takes Bella deep into the woods to a secluded meadow, where he removes his shirt so that she can see his glistening body. (This is the scene that came to Stephenie Meyer in a dream, inspiring her to write the series.) Intoxicated with the sparkling, granite beauty of his perfect body, Bella refuses to believe he would ever hurt her. She already knows he is a vampire by this time. He has warned her repeatedly that he could kill her and admitted that he struggles with a constant desire to do just that. Edward then drops his careful façade of civility, allowing Bella to see just how much danger she is in with him. He tells her that everything about him, including his appearance, his voice, and his fragrance, are designed to attract human prey. He then demonstrates his speed and strength, breaking a huge tree and rushing through the meadow. Edward warns Bella that nothing she could do would protect her from him, that she is utterly defenseless in the face of his thirst (*Twilight*, 259–64). As Bella listens to the threat, his eyes are locked on hers, like a snake's on a bird, and she is terrified, unable to move. (The movie version of *Twilight* significantly changes Edward's threats and removes Bella's fear of Edward's violence. In the movie she says she fears only that she will lose him.)

The first time Bella goes to the Cullens' home, Edward shows her his room, a beautiful space used more for listening to music than anything else, for he does not require sleep. Edward tells Bella his "prodigal son" story, explaining that early in his vampire days he rebelled against Carlisle's animal blood–only rule. After awhile he came to his senses and realized he hated what he had become: a monster and a murderer. He returned to Carlisle and changed his ways. As Bella listens to the story, she again tells Edward that she is not afraid of him, that she knows he would never hurt her, no matter how much he worries otherwise. In response Edward growls, grabs her, throws both of them into the wall and over the furniture, protecting her from actual physical harm but deliber-ately trying to frighten her (*Twilight*, 345). The reader knows that Edward wants Bella to be aware of the real danger in their rela-tionship and that he cares about her well-being. Yet this "caring" behavior is distressingly similar to the show of physical force that batterers use to coerce their partners into compliance.

As the story progresses, the Cullen family agree that Bella's request to be changed into a vampire should be honored. As the family votes yes, Edward flies into a rage, breaking expensive items in the adjacent family living room. He then rushes back into the room with Bella and his family, where he grips Bella violently by the jaw so that she can barely speak. He uses physical force to express his fury at her choice. This scene is one of many violent or disturbing sequences that were cut from the movie version. In general, Edward's anger is seriously downplayed in the mov-ies, making him much more gentle and reasonable than in the books. As we will see in a moment, the fact that readers know that Edward's control and intimidation are partly "for Bella's own good" only makes the normalization of abuse in this story all the more destructive.

When Bella and Edward finally get married, Bella is still human. During their first sexual encounter Edward destroys the furniture, bedding, and Bella's clothing. Their wedding night leaves her covered with bruises. He cannot help himself because he is a vampire. It is all he can do to keep from killing her. This brutality is acceptable to Bella; in fact, she can't wait for more and desperately tries to tempt Edward into further sexual encounters during their honeymoon. The only thing that worries her is whether Edward enjoyed himself (*Breaking Dawn*, 87–98). Because Bella is so insecure about her own worth and her greatest fear is losing Edward, she is willing to endure anything, including sexual violence, if that will please him and keep him close.

Control

A common fallacy about abuse is that the violent partner simply loses his temper or has too much to drink and becomes violent, so that the episodes of violence are isolated rather than systemic. The truth is that control is the core issue for abusers, so they use everything from sweet talk to stalking to maintain power over their partners. Control is what underlies the Jekyll-and-Hyde phenomenon. Edward uses against Bella most of the methods of control that are common to abusive men.

From their first conversation Edward is frustrated that he can't tell what Bella is thinking. While this is flattering to Bella, who is excited that Edward cares about her thoughts, it should be a warning flag to her. One of the signs of abuse developing in a relationship is that the controlling partner demands to know everything the victim is doing, whom she is talking to, and what she is thinking. Abusers cannot abide the victim's having her own friends, conversations, or thoughts beyond the abuser's control.

As Edward and Bella move forward into romance, Edward criticizes Bella for "editing" her thoughts and being selective about what she shares about what she is thinking. He says it makes him insane not to be able to read her mind (*Twilight*, 198, 208). Later, when Jacob and Edward compete for Bella's attention, Edward again tells Bella that she should reveal all her thoughts to him, that he resents her having private thoughts. When she reaches out to him, a few minutes later, asking for sex to let him know how she feels about him, his response is rage. He grabs her wrists, pins them to her sides, and clamps his hand over her mouth so she can't talk or make demands. This leaves Bella hurt and humiliated (*Eclipse*, 441). The message to her is that if she wants Edward's affection, she has to let him invade her mind and fully control their sexual relationship.

When Edward grills Bella about her life, wanting to know every little detail, she refers to his questions as psychoanalysis and cross-examination (*Twilight*, 229–31). His questions are intrusive, but she indulges him anyway, ignoring her own intuitions about his boundary-violating potential. Edward readily answers Bella's questions in turn, but her questions are less intrusive, more cautious and respectful.

One of the major reasons an abuser demands to know the victim's constant whereabouts, conversations, and thoughts is that he is pathologically jealous. He is convinced that his partner is untrustworthy and is going to betray him. He isolates her from friends, family, and especially other men in order to prevent her from sharing her affection with others. He is narcissistic, demanding to be the center of attention for his partner at all times.

Edward is jealous of Bella's friendships with high school boys, even though she obviously adores Edward and finds the other high school students boring. Edward tells Bella he decided to stalk her in order to "keep her safe," but he says this immediately after telling her how sexually attractive she is to all the other boys (*Twilight*, 211). He angrily confesses to her that he feels jealous of Mike (*Twilight*, 302–4). From the beginning of their relationship Edward puts increasing pressure on Bella to let him drive her everywhere and to stop driving her own vehicle. He makes excuses for his demand by saying that her truck isn't safe (when it is), that Bella is too accident-prone to drive herself, or that she drives too slowly and he yearns to be behind the wheel (*Twilight*, 103, 228). These are classic controller moves.

At one point in *Eclipse* Edward actually pays his sister Alice to kidnap Bella whenever he goes hunting so that Bella can't slip away to see Jacob (*Eclipse*, 145–51). And Alice, who should know better, goes along with it, delighted with her payment—a Porsche (*Eclipse*, 145). Edward says he is protecting Bella from "unstable werewolves," but the fact is that he is jealous. Bella is no more at risk with Jacob than she is with Edward. Bella knows at some level that Edward's behavior is "psychotic and controlling," as she admits in *Eclipse*, but she goes along with it anyway (145–51). When Jacob tells Bella he saw a television program about abusive relationships and suggests that Bella should be worried about Edward's treatment of her, Bella shrugs him off (*Eclipse*, 224). *Eclipse* also includes a scene in which Bella seeks Edward's permission to go to La Push, as if he has the right to determine her movements (230–231). One of the reasons Bella is so vulnerable to paternalism from Edward is that she has grown up essentially fatherless and, in many ways, motherless.

Stalking is another method that abusers use to intimidate, control, and isolate their partners. In addition to literally following their victims when they go to work, school, shopping, or errands, stalkers might hack into victims' e-mail, secretly listen in on telephone conversations, hide video cameras around the house to keep tabs on what is happening, and telephone victims constantly when they are not with them. This kind of behavior may seem harmless at first, an expression of affection or protection, and as in Bella's case may make the victim feel especially treasured. But stalking is never a loving or respectful action. It is a form of aggression and control.

When Bella realizes for the first time that Edward is stalking her (not an unusual activity for a vampire, granted), she is *happy* about it (*Twilight*, 174–75). For weeks he has been following her around, watching her, and even sneaking into her room at night to watch her sleep. Bella describes herself as hopelessly addicted to Edward, so much so that she is flattered instead of frightened by his stalking. She seems to realize that stalking is a dangerous behavior and a violation of appropriate boundaries, but she has given herself over to him anyway (*Twilight*, 292). When Edward admits to Bella that he has been sneaking into her room at night to watch her sleep, Bella is at first stunned, then anxious. Rather than worrying about a blood-thirsty vampire looming over her while she sleeps, she worries only that he has heard her talking in her sleep about her obsession over him (*Twilight*, 292–94).

When Edward is moody or controlling toward Bella, she often takes responsibility for his behavior. For example, early in their relationship when Edward is conflicted about Bella, he tells her they can't be friends. Bella, instead of deciding that Edward has issues, believes he can't be friends with her because he is perfect and beautiful while she is dull and clumsy. When he flies into a rage at her because she hasn't told anyone she is hiking alone with him in the mountains, she only cares about protecting him (*Twilight*, 255). She admits that she didn't tell anyone because she didn't want Edward to get in trouble if he killed her. This is the logic of abuse victims who think, "If I just fry the chicken next time instead of baking it, he won't hit me. I should have known better."

Bella realizes that it is unhealthy to give Edward so much power over her, but she does it anyway because his aura of danger only makes her more fascinated with him (*Twilight*, 67, 74–75, 93). She says that she is "consumed" with him—note the eating language—and that her obsession is "stupid, stupid, stupid." But she just can't help herself. She is, like so many women in unhealthy relationships, enmeshed with Edward, referring to herself as a satellite that moves around Edward, the planet. She constantly adjusts herself to his gravitational pull, adapting to his demands, caving to his control (*Eclipse*, 68). Bella is so entangled that she panics when Edward distances himself from her, causing her to beg him to reveal what angers him so she doesn't trigger whatever makes him suddenly withdraw (*Twilight*, 274). Such "walking on eggshells" is a chronic way of life for victims of abuse whose boundaries have all but disappeared.

Edward utterly controls the relationship, everything from who drives the car to how much physical touch transpires and when, where, and why they get married. It is only after Bella becomes a vampire that any kind of equality grows in their relationship. We'll learn more about that later.

There is just one more interesting detail about Edward as the boyfriend every parent dreads. Not only does he manifest most of the signs of a batterer, but as Susan Vaught demonstrates, he also fits the profile of someone with antisocial personality disorder, more commonly known as a sociopath. In order to be clinically diagnosed with antisocial personality disorder a person has to exhibit at least three of seven criteria. Vaught explains how Edward fits all seven.[8]

Some readers tell me that it's going too far to describe Edward as abusive, much less as a sociopath. "He did those things to protect Bella," they protest. "He's in love with her." Their defensiveness of Edward is not about his abuse but about his motives. Since his rages and crazy behavior arise out of love, they reason, it isn't the same as if he acted out of hate.

Therein lies the problem.

Ironically, part of what makes the Twilight novels' messages of violence against women so untenable is that the reader eventually learns that Edward has some legitimate reasons for part of his abusive and controlling behavior. Those reasons all have to do with protecting Bella from real danger. Edward is angry that he can't read Bella's thoughts, for example, because he literally can read everyone else's, a gift that helps him protect those he loves. Edward begins driving her everywhere partly to protect her from bad vampires. He resists physical intimacy with her because he wants to protect her from his own cravings. All of these elements help the reader to "forgive" Edward for his abuse as the story unfolds. The problem is that abusive men use manipulation, "reasonable" explanations, and other maneuvers—including claims to protect and watch over their victims—to keep their victims confused and under obligation to forgive and endure unacceptable behavior.

Don't Call It Love

The theme of violence against women at the hands of their intimate partners runs throughout all four Twilight novels and is even more pronounced in Meyer's stand-alone book *The Host*. From relatively mild boundary violations to gang rape, most of the women characters in Twilight have been victimized. Most disturbingly, Meyer treats this theme in ways that normalize such violence. As mentioned earlier, Esme, Rosalie, Emily, and Alice have all been victimized. Of these three, Rosalie's story, which took place in the 1930s, most clearly reproduces fallacies about what causes rape.

Rosalie explains that her fiancé and his friends had been out drinking when they found her walking down a street at night. Overcome with desire for her because of her beauty, they gang-raped her to the point that she was near death when Carlisle found her. Even as a "resurrected" vampire with more than human perspective, Rosalie thought that the sexual assault that took her life was initiated because of her beauty and desirability (*Eclipse*, 132). While she exacted vengeance on her assailants, torturing and murdering them after she was a vampire, she still saw her own body as a partial cause for what happened to her. Rosalie describes the attack to Bella:

> "What did I tell you, John," Royce crowed, grabbing my arm and pulling me closer. "Isn't she lovelier than all your Georgia peaches?" The man named John was dark-haired and suntanned. He looked me over like I was a horse he was buying. "It's hard to tell," he drawled slowly. "She's all covered up." (*Eclipse*, 159)

This is not the message readers need to hear. Rape is a crime of violence, not an act of sexual intimacy. Rape victims are never to blame for the violence of their perpetrators. Rape is never excusable because of a woman's clothing, beauty, vulnerability, location, speech, or any other aspect of her person. There is never a justification for rape.

My greatest disappointment with the Twilight series is Stephenie Meyer's thematic representation of violence against women in a way that minimizes and normalizes abuse. No matter how wonderful it is that Meyer promotes sexual abstinence before marriage, a fact that elicits high praise from some religious commentators, she offers a terrible message about violence against women at the hands of their intimate partners. The saturation of this narrative with violence against women is lost on some of the religious leaders who extol the series for its biblical commitment to chastity. Dave Roberts, for example, describes the brutal wedding night as "overenthusiastic sex."[9] Roberts also says the "moral center of the story" is found not in the relationship Bella has with Edward or anyone else but in the interplay between Edward and Carlisle.[10] One wonders if Roberts considers justice for women to be a "biblical" value.

A Table for Two

Being alone is second only to death in being the worst possible fate for the characters in Twilight. Throughout the novels the unhappy characters are the ones without mates. When Edward thinks Bella has drowned, he quickly decides to take his own life. It would be better to die, he reasons, than to be alone (*New Moon*, 19). But this series has a happy ending. With the exception of poor Leah, as the story draws to a close everyone else has a partner. Edward has Bella. Jacob has little Renesmee. Even Charlie finds happiness again; with Bella out of the sheriff's house, the widow Sue Clearwater begins to cook for Charlie, and soon they are in love. Almost everyone enjoys a table for two.

But are these romance-novel endings Christian? Are they healthy? It is true that God tells Adam, "It is not good for man to be alone" (Gen. 2:18). There is biblical precedent for the basic unit of the family, which is the couple. Yet the notion that singleness is almost as loathsome as death absolutely conflicts with the gospel, including the words of Jesus, who was himself a single man. Jesus said to his disciples that some people have a vocation of being "eunuchs" for the sake of the kingdom (Matt. 19:12). Singleness for those individuals is a blessing and a gift. It is a way of life that participates in the kingdom of God for the sake of the world. It is missional. It is why men and women who are vowed members of most traditional monastic orders, for example, do not marry. Their commitment is to the kingdom of God.

Even though some adults choose to remain single for the sake of the kingdom of God, there are other legitimate reasons that adults might remain single. In addition to simply not finding a suitable mate, a large number of us will one day be widowed or divorced. Does this mean that we have to be miserable or that we are defective? Hardly. Does marriage guarantee happiness? Apparently not, according to statistics. About fifty percent of marriages in the United States end in divorce, and statistics from the Barna group demonstrate that divorce rates are even higher among evangelical Christians than among atheists and agnostics.[11]

Jesus made it clear that what leads to "the good life" in the kingdom of God hinges on a completely different set of values. Other than his words about eunuchs and divorce (which we already considered), Jesus' guidelines for the good life are virtually silent about marriage and family. Instead, he boldly states that in the kingdom of God we have mothers, brothers, and sisters in the family of faith. He refuses to sexualize women or prescribe domestic gender roles for women or men. On the contrary, he praises women and men alike for knowing and doing the will of God.

The one example that we have in the New Testament of a "Christian family" is that of Joseph, Mary, and Jesus. (I realize they were Jewish, but in relation to Jesus as the Christ, it's all right to think of them as Christian, too.) Isn't it striking that the most notable feature of Joseph as husband is that he surrenders his own dreams in order to make a way for Mary to fulfill her vocation? No wonder Jesus is a liberator of women.

As Beth Felker Jones discusses in her book about Twilight, even the best marriages are riddled with human frailty and disappointments. To romanticize and idealize marriage is idolatrous, and to discount and marginalize the gift of singleness goes against the teachings of both Jesus and Paul.[12] The very idea that marriage is about cleaving to your one true "soul mate" contributes to infidelity and the breakup of marriages, she writes, because it is so easy when the relationship is rocky to find someone better who might be the "real" soul mate.[13] The idea that being part of a couple is necessary in order to be happy and fulfilled robs people of freedom and leads to many forms of oppression.

By now you may be wondering if I think there is *anything* good in Edward and Bella's relationship. The answer is a resounding yes. In chapter 4 we will take a close look at the deeper meanings of their desire for one another and why this part of the story is profound. But first we need to think about gender, because so many of the problems in this story stem from the stereotyped gender roles that Meyer creates.

Chapter Three

Is Twilight Bad News for Girls?

First of all, we have to acknowledge that something about Bella resonates with girls around the world. At the time of this writing the Twilight series has been translated into more than forty languages. Even when readers dislike Bella (and lots of them do, as we'll see in a moment), there are many ways in which she is Everygirl, especially in how she awakens to love and to her own sexuality. When she is around Edward, Bella experiences exactly the same feelings girls everywhere have when falling in love for the first time—the electrification, the obsession, the amazement. She can't believe that anyone could be so gorgeous, so perfect as her Edward. No one has ever loved the way she loves. These are feelings girls understand.

Bella also reflects the tension girls around the world experience between accepting and resisting socially constructed gender roles. Though every culture is different, there is enough about this dilemma in Bella's life to resonate with readers everywhere. As she moves through the harrowing adventures of the series toward the final climax in *Breaking Dawn*, Bella comes of age and discovers her own power. Though some readers complain that it takes too long for her to get her groove on, in the end she finally does. She grows up.

Bella the Pathetic

Let's get this over with right now, okay? Lots of readers can't stand Bella even though they love the books. Why? Quite honestly it's because through much of the story she's pathetic. Until Bella lives into her power, she is like a slapstick comedian without the humor. She trips over her own feet, breaks things, knocks people's books on the floor, and gives herself a lump on the shin, all the while meditating on how loathsome her life has become. Gym is her personal hell because of the daily indignities she suffers there (*Twilight*, 17, 26). Bella is unable to hold a badminton racquet without hitting herself in the head (*Twilight*, 221). Mike, her male classmate, automatically plays Bella's position as well as his own because she is such a klutz, and she doesn't even see the insult in this action (*Twilight*, 51).

Bella's dysfunction extends beyond the physical realm to her emotional and intellectual self. While trying to decide whether and how to confront Edward about his bizarre mood swings, Bella confesses that she knows she'll never really do it because she is so timid that she makes "the Cowardly Lion look like the Terminator" (*Twilight*, 30). Linked to her scaredy-cat self is her history of fainting spells. Apparently these spells are precipitated by fear, not a medical condition. After fainting because of a biology assignment in which students study a wee drop of their own blood, Bella is exhausted and says that fainting spells always wear her out (*Twilight*, 101). Always? How often does this happen? In *Twilight*, the fainting episode is resolved by Edward carrying her to the school nurse, a rescue that establishes a regular pattern of a strong male saving the damsel in distress.

Bella is unable to figure out how to fasten her own seatbelt in the Cullens' monster Jeep. It has too many large, masculine buckles, so she needs Edward to help her (*Twilight*, 360). Worse than these gender stereotypes of physical weakness, Bella is intellectually lacking as well. She hates trigonometry. She says she has to work ten times as hard on math as she does on English, just to squeak through with an A-minus (*Twilight*, 17; *New Moon*, 98). The only reason Bella is competent in biology is because she is repeating course material in Forks that she just covered in Phoenix. Even her biology teacher, Mr. Banner, assumes that Edward must be helping Bella in class and that she couldn't possibly be so smart on her own (*Twilight*, 47, 51). Here Meyer mimics an old gender stereotype that refuses to die despite strong evidence that girls are as talented in the "hard" disciplines of math and science as they are in "soft" disciplines such as English.

Moreover, Bella is deficient in social skills. Early on in *Twilight* we learn that our heroine has never had any friends other than her flaky mother (*Twilight*, 10–11). She simply doesn't know how to relate to others, nor is she interested in learning how. Bella is like the awkward child in elementary school who doesn't play well with others but gets on famously with hamsters and dogs.

What does this less-than-wonderful profile have to do with gender? Everything. Bella is an extreme version of a girl who feels inferior, a girl who doesn't fit, and this feeling is a certitude that is thrust on most of us girls and women in the United States well before we hit puberty. (For a powerful and well-documented study of the culturally induced, widespread phenomenon of depression and low self-esteem among adolescent girls, see Mary Pipher's *Reviving Ophelia*.)[1]

The feelings of self-doubt, shame, and inadequacy come from being indoctrinated with the message that we are not beautiful enough, graceful enough, thin enough, curvy enough, talented enough, athletic enough, rich enough, or sexy enough to actually count. We girls and women are given a thousand messages a day from television, movies, magazines, and the Web that we are deficient. Our thighs are too big, our teeth too yellow, our hair too thin, our eyelashes too pale. Bella is all that. No wonder so many readers love to hate Bella. She is us when we are enslaved to the lie. She is the socially constructed false self that we hate but from which we find it so hard to escape.

Bella the Drama Queen

The theme of escape is what keeps this drama rolling. Every time you turn the page in the Twilight saga somebody's on the run— especially Bella. She seems to be dead set on hurting herself, first to get away from her pain and then to sacrifice herself to save others. We see this self-destructive impulse throughout *New Moon*, after the accident-prone Bella has suffered a paper cut at the birthday party the Cullens throw for her. Her delicious, fragrant blood—Edward's personal brand of heroin—splashes down onto the clean, pale floor. All hell breaks loose. Jasper instinctively goes for the blood; Edward and Emmett go for Jasper; and even sweet Esme has to leave the room lest she be driven to feed.

Edward hauls Bella out into the creepy woods where he announces the end of their romance and says that it was a mistake for him to be with her. He is absolutely cold in his delivery. Then he disappears along with all of the Cullens, who are on the run so that their cover won't be blown in Forks. Bella, overwhelmed with grief, runs deep into the forest, which is fraught with dangers of many kinds, not least of which are nonvegetarian vampires. Naturally, she trips and falls, sinks into a stupor, becomes hypothermic, and lies there in the rain hoping to die.

Hours later she is rescued by Sam Uley, a member of the Quileute tribe (*New Moon*, 72–76). (At this point in the story Bella does not know the Quileutes' secret, that Sam is the alpha of a pack of werewolves.) Once home again Bella descends into a funk that lasts for months. Outwardly she goes through the motions of daily life, but inwardly she is dead. She feels completely responsible for the Cullens' need to run. If she hadn't been so careless, she tells herself, if she hadn't cut her finger, everything would still be wonderful. She concludes that everything bad that has happened is her fault.

Bella's self-blaming would be beyond ridiculous if it weren't so true to how many girls feel when the one they love dumps them and disappears. Most of us at some point have wanted to sink into the earth and have the rain wash us into oblivion. It is the feeling of rejection and despair, of losing your first true love.

As Bella continues in this state of depression, her father urges her to rekindle her friendship with the Quileute boy Jacob Black and to get back in touch with some of her girlfriends. Either she gets back out into the world, he threatens, or he's sending her back to her mother. Rousing herself from her torpor, Bella goes to town with a friend from school. There she sees a group of motorcycle thugs in front of One-Eyed Pete's bar. She remembers the time she nearly got mugged by a similar group of men, but Edward saved her. This memory sparks in her a desire to approach the seedy crowd, a monumentally stupid act. As she begins to move toward them, she "hears" Edward's voice warning her not to do it. Whether she imagines his voice or he somehow does contact her psychically is not clear. For a moment the depressed fog lifts, giving her relief (*New Moon*, 109–11). Out of this experience Bella decides to continue putting herself in danger in order to experience the momentary joy of hearing Edward's imagined voice.

This unleashes a sequence of risky behaviors on Bella's part, including jumping from a cliff into the frigid waters of the Pacific, which causes Jacob to have to rescue her, and then riding a motorcycle at high speeds and crashing it. During both of these near-death experiences Bella hears Edward. The adrenaline rush and his voice are like a drug to Bella, a brief respite from her pain (*New Moon*, 109–11, 127–28).

Bella's pattern of behavior is very much like cutting, a self-mutilating compulsion that is at epidemic levels among adolescent girls in the United States.[2] Girls who self-mutilate do so in order to express pain and rage that they have otherwise "numbed." For a moment the cut, burn, or other injury creates a vivid pain that they can feel. Cutting is an unhealthy way for someone to be able to feel again. While many who injure themselves deliberately are survivors of sexual abuse and other forms of trauma, not all have that history. What is common to those who cut themselves is a need to feel relief from deadening emotional pain; the paradox is that relief comes through the pain of self-injury.

Bella takes other risks as well. Though she knows from seeing Emily's scarred visage that being with werewolves is far from safe, Bella prefers them to human company. Even Alice chides her about this after she returns to check on Bella, saying that anyone else would be better off when the vampires left town, but not our Bella (*New Moon*, 387). Bella is like good girls who get top grades, eat their vegetables, and don't smoke but are hopelessly drawn to date convicted felons. The nice, responsible boys are boring.

As Bella begins frequent visits with Jacob Black with her father's grateful blessing, she finds herself "settling into another version of herself," one that is more playful and laid back, one that laughs and jokes and actually has fun (*Eclipse*, 101). Many readers like this other Bella better than the original. Taking on this playful persona helps Bella to emerge from her depression. In this way it is good, saving her from potentially dire outcomes. It is part of adolescent development for girls to try on different ways of relating to people, an important aspect of individuating from their parents. Yet there is a disturbing, dysfunctional side to Bella's alternate self. It reflects what can be called the chameleon syndrome, a sign of insecurity and unhealthy boundaries in girls who are struggling with shame. They automatically try to become what they think the significant other wants. They'll do anything to keep the other from disappearing.

This leads us to another problem with Bella. She uses Jake deliberately (*New Moon*, 162–218). Bella knows she will never love Jacob as much as she loves Edward. He will never *really* be her significant other, but she strings him along anyway, offering just enough closeness to keep him coming back for more. Jacob is by far the healthier and more honest of the two, and judging from the fervent advocacy of "Team Jacob," plenty of fans think Jacob is hands-down hotter than Edward. Bella's ongoing use of Jacob as a "fix" for Edward's absence, along with her denial of her own real feelings for him, embody yet another negative female stereotype—the two-timing tease who says no when she means yes. Bella uses Jake as a rebound from Edward, a means of escape from her loneliness and grief.

Bella also presents a troubling model for girls in her relentless disregard for her own body. In yet another example of Bella's self-destructive tendencies, she is drawn to identify with a legendary Quileute woman who sacrifices herself for her people. When Bella hears the story of the Third Wife and the "cold woman" (a vampire) at a Quileute ceremonial campfire, she is captivated by the idea of the wife plunging a knife into her own belly to attract the vampire's attention and give her husband and sons an opening to take the cold woman down. Later on when there is a showdown with Victoria and her army of newborns, Bella tries to reenact the Third Wife's sacrifice, slicing her arm open to try to help Edward and Seth, rendering assistance that they actually do not need. They are already winning the fight. Bella's action complicates matters and puts them at greater risk (although in the movie version her self-mutilation helps) (*Eclipse*, 264, 539).

Bella embodies several negative messages about women in this vignette. She is passive, convinced that the only useful thing she can do is to give up her blood in order to help her friends, rather than active, taking an offensive position against the enemy in tandem with her friends. Moreover, Bella identifies with a Quileute wife who doesn't even have a name, an anonymous woman who bleeds to death so that her husband and sons (who do have names) can carry on the family line. The only thing that makes the Quileute woman valuable is her death. Her life doesn't count. What causes Bella to identify with the Third Wife is precisely the woman's insignificance, weakness, and unremarkable life other than her suicide mission. Bella sees herself in that same light, so she decides to do the only thing she can imagine herself capable of: bleeding.

Please Want Me

Bella is completely insecure about Edward's feelings for her no matter what he says or does. When Bella tells Edward that she is so ordinary that she is worthless compared to him, Edward is stunned, then angry. He chides her for her lack of awareness of her own beauty, telling her that he has been reading the other boys' minds and they all think Bella is very sexy (*Twilight*, 210). She doesn't believe him.

The first time Bella goes to the Cullen home, she obsesses about whether they will accept her in light of her obvious lack of grace and beauty compared to all of them. It doesn't occur to her that what she should really be worried about is whether they are hungry. In her insecurity, she keeps comparing herself to Edward, who is a "powerful motorcycle" while she is a "broken tricycle" (*Eclipse*, 233).

Even on their wedding day Bella is pitiful. Our Bella marches grimly to the altar, convinced of her shabbiness, refusing to look in the mirror after Alice works her girly magic on the bride (*Breaking Dawn*, 57). As she catches a glimpse of herself reflected in a window, Bella can scarcely recognize the dusky beauty she sees looking back. Right up until the time she is changed to a vampire on her deathbed, Bella worries that she won't have what it takes to "hold" Edward once she is no longer human (*New Moon*, 523). She just doesn't think she's good enough. And she thinks the real reason Edward is so hesitant to change her is that he, too, thinks he will lose interest in her after she stops smelling so deliciously of human blood (*Eclipse*, 273).

To find out more about how women's self-esteem affects marriages, I recently talked about this issue with a therapist friend who does a lot of marriage counseling. She told me that she often asks couples what would make them happier. Many of the women say that if they just lost twenty pounds all would be well. They would be fulfilled and their marriage would improve. The husbands, according to my friend, usually protest saying, "I love you just the way you are. You don't have to lose twenty pounds." But the wives never believe the husbands. They believe the airbrushed images on magazine covers instead, standards of female beauty that they can never achieve but to which they constantly compare themselves. "What these women don't get," my friend concluded in frustration, "is that most men are much deeper than that. Most men care about a woman's personality, her soul, her whole self, whether she has a sense of humor, that sort of thing. And by the way, lots of men like a woman with curves. They like the softness. But most of the women I see refuse to believe these things." Edward asks Bella essentially the same question my friend asks her clients: "Why can you believe a lie but not the truth" about yourself? (*New Moon*, 511)

Caretaking and Other Problems

One of the great ironies of this story and of life is that we women are simultaneously told that we need to be taken care of because we are vulnerable and weak, *and* that we have to take care of everyone in our lives except ourselves because it's our job. It makes little sense, but many of us have believed it anyway. Bella certainly does.

From the time she was a wee lass Bella has been taking care of her mother (*Twilight*, 4). After she moves to Forks, she takes care of her dad, cooking and cleaning, the picture of domesticity. Lord knows what Charlie did all those years before she showed up! Bella moves into the kitchen right away, making sure Charlie gets a balanced diet and his laundry gets done. She mothers him (*Twilight*, 31, 295, and too many other references to enumerate here). Charlie expects this from her, too; when he comes home from work, he asks where supper is, like an overgrown kid with a sheriff's badge.

At the same time that she functions like a superresponsible adult taking care of her parents, Bella is treated like a child by Edward and other men. Bella is forever being carried around in some guy's arms because she fainted, broke a bone, crashed, nearly drowned, ran into the woods on a cold night, or swooned. Edward rocks Bella to sleep in a rocker, like a little child, then carries her downstairs to breakfast after the first night she discovers he stays all night every night with her (*Twilight*, 314–15). She loves this. It is the kind of fatherly attention she has never had and for which she is starved. She and lots of young readers are vulnerable to controlling, paternalistic men for this very reason. We can understand why Bella would agree to being childlike around men and would cooperate with their caretaking of her, but it is not a healthy message for readers about the way women should relate to men. A loving relationship is one that is mutual, not paternalistic, not controlling. A woman needs a partner, not a daddy, for her significant other. Ironically, Edward's paternalism is literal—he is old enough to be her great-grandfather.

This is the bad news about gender in Twilight relative to Bella. Before we go to the good news, and I promise there is some, we need also to consider the bad news about gender coming from some of the other female characters in this story, the vampires and the Quileutes.

Note the ways that Esme, Alice, and Rosalie are often one-dimensional and stereotyped even as vampires. Esme is a gentle mom who cooks delicious food for others and likes to refurbish historic homes. Don't get me wrong, I'm all for being a great mom and having architectural appreciation. But this is a traditional, overly domestic stereotype of an upper-middle-class white woman. Wouldn't Esme be more interesting if, for example, she also worked for immigration rights, or if she were a beekeeper? What if she wrote best-selling novels about vampires? Wouldn't readers be able to identify with her more and look up to her? She has all that time on her immortal hands. Couldn't she do something rewarding and useful in addition to taking care of her family, all of whom are perfectly able to care for themselves because they are adults and the world's deadliest predators?

Alice is a Cosmo girl, totally into fashion and shopping. Though she does have an impressive clairvoyant gift, she is the brunette Barbie of the undead world, dancing here, prancing there, her voice tinkling like fairy bells. We are relieved when she helps tear off James's head, just to know she has chutzpah, but these moments of gutsy action are few and far between. Alice is by far the most developed of the female vampire characters, with greater complexity in her personality and role. But even Alice is doomed to female stereotypes. Her most outstanding gift, clairvoyance, is a stereotypically submissive one in which she passively receives mental impressions of the future. In contrast, her partner, Jasper, uses his gift, the ability to manipulate emotions, to change the emotional climate of an entire group of people. He is an actor rather than a receiver of others' actions.

Then there is Rosalie, the vindictive ice queen who lives in the past and boasts to Bella about thirsting for blood. She goes around brooding most of the time over the fact that she can't have a baby. When she isn't thinking about her sad lot in the universe, she relishes memories of torturing and mutilating her killers, which makes *us* thankful she can't have a baby. At times we wonder what Emmett sees in her, but then we remember she is the auto mechanic for the family, something that makes us cut her some slack and heave a sigh of relief. Rosalie gives Bella the cold shoulder. She only begins to relate to her in the fourth novel because of the baby.

Let's not forget the bad ones, either, Jane and Victoria, both of whom are sadists. Victoria's little-girl voice makes her sexy to men, but it masks an utter ruthlessness. (What does that say about men, by the way?) Victoria uses one of her newborn male vampires, Riley, as a lover and a weapon. Without James her existence devolves into a narrative of vengeance against Edward. She creates Riley, who then helps her to produce an army of newborns who advance on Forks to attack the Cullens. Riley thinks Victoria really loves him, but he is just a tool for her.[3]

Jane is scarcely more than a child but with the heart of Count de Sade. She is the most powerful torturer in the Volturi. By choosing a preadolescent girl to represent the height of Volturi depravity, Meyer reinforces the stereotype that if women are given power they will use it to destroy others. Jane is a worst-case scenario.

The wives of the Volturi are mere wisps of smoke who stay in the towers for hundreds of years, having no names and no life. What do they do for centuries, up there in the towers? We can imagine them knitting ghostly shawls and sipping their afternoon blood from Royal Albert teacups. They are nonentities, a stereotyped message about old women that is enforced constantly through television, movies, advertising, and the multibillion dollar cosmetic surgery industry.

And we've already noted that Leah, the one female werewolf, is a mess in this story precisely because she is androgynous. No one reading these books would want to be Leah. Note to readers: Gender is not fluid in the world of Stephenie Meyer. Girls wear pink and boys wear blue, and characters who muddy the waters can forget about having a Good Life.

Emily, the girlfriend of Sam Uley the werewolf, is a rustic Quileute version of Esme. She would be a great country music writer. She stands by her man, cooks for all the wolf boys, tends her garden, cleans her cabin, and is thankful. There's also the bit about how she stays hidden away in the woods with disfiguring scars that Sam accidentally inflicted when he was out of control in her presence. Emily's world is entirely privatized, domestic, and dominated by men.

No women in the Twilight saga are single, strong, intelligent, *and* happy. We see no women occupied in a profession that is good for humanity; no women who are married, mothers, *and* have an interesting and meaningful work life outside the home; and no women who have a sense of humor, whether they are vampires, werewolves, or humans. Not one.

Bella Gets Her Groove On

The good news—and yes, thankfully there is some to report in the gender department—is that Bella changes. Once Bella becomes a vampire through the purgatory-like process of conversion (*Breaking Dawn*, 369–86), a transformation we will explore more thoroughly in chapter 5, she is amazing. No longer is she clumsy, pathetic, or lame. For the remaining 368 pages of this four-volume saga Bella is ravishingly beautiful, confident, intelligent, secure, sexually powerful, stronger physically than Emmett, fearless, and gifted with a rare ability to shield herself and others from the supernatural gifts of hostile vampires. She has preternatural self-control over bodily hungers. She is wise.

One of the final, most satisfying reversals is that Bella also becomes humble about her mother. (After all, humility toward others in their weakness, including toward her own mother, Renee, is a mark of true beauty.) As the Cullens and their friends prepare for what could be their annihilation at the hands of the Volturi, Alice and Jasper disappear. For strategic reasons they do not let the rest of the family know where they have gone. As Bella ponders the dire circumstances and longs to see Alice, her child Renesmee comforts her. Bella realizes in amazement that the mother-daughter bond has for a moment been reversed between her and Renesmee, something she never thought could or should happen. She remembers how she had always comforted and cared for Renee, her mother. Now in this moment she realizes that there are times when it is good and right for a daughter to comfort her mother. Although this point remains undeveloped in the story, it's clear that Bella has eaten a bit of humble pie and developed a new compassion for her mother.

In these ways Bella the Vampire presents the reader with a hopeful if fanciful role model of female strength and wisdom.

She actually embodies some of the qualities of the wise woman of Proverbs 31:10–31:

> She girds herself with strength,
>   and makes her arms strong.
> . . . .
> Her lamp does not go out at night.
> . . . .
> Strength and dignity are her clothing,
>   and she laughs at the time to come.
>   (vv. 17, 18b, 25)

Though the Bible's Wisdom figure is something of an enigma, representing in some ways a feminine image of God and in other ways the personification of wisdom as a woman, for millennia women have had the wise woman of Proverbs 31 as a role model. That is, "Lady Wisdom" has been taken as a literal model for ideal womanhood. Though many preachers use this text on Mother's Day, a close examination of what it really says would be enough to make the hair stand up on patriarchal necks.

First of all, the wise woman of Proverbs is a woman of strength. The Hebrew phrase used here for strength is, in our socially constructed understandings of gender, usually considered masculine—sexual power and military prowess. That is, the wise woman has the ability to fight and win, and she has the life-giving power of healthy sexuality rightly expressed. She uses her incredible strength in ways that bless the whole community, not just herself or her immediate family.

The wise woman of Proverbs is defined neither by her husband's nor her children's achievements. She is defined by God and has a self. She is fully human. Though she loves her family and is a responsible wife and mother, there is much more to her than her family. In fact, her family sometimes basks in the reflected glow of public recognition that the wise woman receives for her contributions to the community.

She has a life outside the four walls of her home. She works, has money of her own that she earns and spends, and is wise in how she invests both her time and her money. She has a life that matters, and everyone around her knows it. No one would accuse her of being self-centered, nor would anyone say she is lacking in self-esteem. She has *shalom*. The wise woman is a gifted, intelligent spiritual teacher not just of her children and other women but also the community at large. Like the prophet Deborah, the wise woman is sought out for her spiritual wisdom. She is highly honored because of this.

The Proverbs 31 woman is not anxious, not a people pleaser, and not afraid of the future or of hardship. She fears God alone, and this gives her great confidence to engage the challenges of daily life. Not overly concerned with her physical appearance, the wise woman understands her beauty in relationship to God. Her strong, fruitful life and her unfading beauty flow from that relationship.

While we do not get to spend enough time with Bella after she is transformed into a vampire, in the last several hundred pages we do see many of the qualities of the wise woman in her. She is girded with strength, both in fighting against injustice and in loving Edward. Her gifts of wisdom and protection are for the whole community, not just her nuclear family. While she is grateful that Edward finds her even more beautiful and desirable than before (and let's face it, she is thankful that she will be eternally young and sexy), Bella feels deep joy in her surprising ability to resist the thirst for human blood and her self-control in the use of her supernatural strength. She is able to let her anger at Volturi injustice fuel her constructive action for the well-being of her community.

Throughout the Twilight novels it is important to ask ourselves, Is this story good news for girls and women? Is it good news for boys and men? In the next chapter we will consider in depth the relationship between Edward and Bella as Stephenie Meyer deliberately plays on the Genesis narrative of creation, sin, and forbidden fruit. There, too, we will see many assumptions about gender that shape the direction of the story.

Part Two

The Gospel according to Twilight

God, Spirituality, and Faith

Chapter Four

Thirst
Forbidden Fruit in Forks

What we really need to know about the Twilight novels, with all their plots, themes, and drama, is that the driving force of this story is desire. This is a tale of unremitting hunger. It is a saga of raw, elemental need and of the lengths to which lovers will go in order to slake their thirst.

Therein lies the spiritual power of the story for those with eyes to see and ears to hear. For as many of the great Christian mystics tell us, all forms of thirst—all experiences of hunger, longing, and need, all the joy and suffering of desire—are rooted in the mystery of the God who is Love. Even when our desires are twisted and broken, if traced back to their original root they lead us home to the Ancient of Days. Each of our thirsts has the potential to reveal something precious to us about God and ourselves, and about the world in which we live. They remind us of the interdependence of life.

Both the essence of holiness and the essence of sin are bound to the central fact of thirst. The lure of temptation is to satisfy a legitimate thirst with means that are destructive. There is always in temptation a suggestion that maybe the forbidden choice won't be so bad, or that it is actually life giving and we've only been duped into thinking that it is wrong. Forbidden fruit is appealing precisely because, in the words of the old song, how can something be so wrong when it *feels* so right?

In the Beginning

The first time any of us experienced thirst, we were just a few hours old. Having emerged from the safe warmth of our mothers' bodies, we encountered a strange new world of light, noise, and, yes, the shock of thirst. Before our eyes could focus we learned to recognize our mother's scent.[1] She was usually the one who slaked our thirst. She wrapped us in soft clothing and held us in her arms, giving us the sweet milk that we craved. At the sound of her voice we felt assurance. Our anxiety turned to anticipation. The milk would soon fill us, and for a little while the thirst would go away.

As much as we thirsted for milk, we thirsted for touch. Every human is born with a need for skin contact—the cuddling and the raspberry kisses our loved ones gave to us. Touch is so important to infants that if there is not enough, they can suffer developmental and emotional abnormalities, including a condition called "failure to thrive."[2] Without loving touch humans can suffer brain damage. We can die.

We were also born with a powerful thirst to belong. To be human is to be communal. God told Adam that it was not good for him to be alone. And it wasn't enough for Adam and Eve to have each other; the animals were part of their community. Moreover, the Bible says that Adam and Eve walked with God in the cool of the evening. They needed human, creaturely, and divine community. Though brief times of solitude are good for all of us, one of our basic human needs is to belong. It is why adolescents from dysfunctional families are so vulnerable to gangs; the gang provides an option for belonging. And it is why solitary confinement is a form of torture, with its deprivation of community.

Finally, we are born with a deep need for significance. We first felt this kind of thirst when we carried our crayon art to our parents, who praised us while fastening our scribbles to the refrigerator. We wanted to be noticed, to be special and cherished. If a baby sister or brother came along many of us felt wildly jealous. The little interloper might steal some of Mom and Dad's affection. Our unique place in the universe might collapse.

So the needs for food, touch, belonging, and significance are primeval, God given. We find these basic thirsts in the story of the creation and fall of the first humans in the Bible. They are also the thirsts of Edward and Bella, whose story draws deliberately from a certain reading of Genesis. Whenever we speak of forbidden fruit we reference, whether intentionally or not, Genesis 1–3 with its many forms of God-given thirst. And let us remember as well that these thirsts are at the core of the intoxication commonly known as "falling in love." Let's think about the various ways the theme of forbidden fruit is found in this story, then explore how Meyer's interpretation of the Genesis narrative plays out in the Twilight saga. Is this interpretation good news for readers?

A Book about Forbidden Fruit

The cover art for *Twilight* features a pair of comely arms emerging from the dark with a luscious red apple, announcing to the shopper a tantalizing read. Moreover, the epigraph that opens the story is Genesis 2:17: "But of the tree of the knowledge of good and evil, thou shalt not eat of it; for in the day that thou eatest thereof thou shalt surely die"(KJV). It is a book about *forbidden fruit*! Who is the tempter, and who is the tempted? Can the hero or heroine resist temptation? Can the shopper resist the juicy promise of the cover? And what does the apple on the cover represent in *Twilight*?

Lots of things. Blood, for starters. If Edward is going to be a good vampire, following the example of Carlisle, there can be no bloodletting with Bella or any other human. Not only is Bella forbidden fruit because she is human; she is also the one Edward loves. He has given his heart to her, so he must not kill her. As the Bible says about Adam and Eve with the forbidden fruit, the day Edward "eats thereof" Bella will die, and their love will be no more. This would lead to his own death, for after Edward falls in love with Bella, he comes to believe that if she should perish, he too must die (*New Moon*, 19). Just like Romeo and Juliet. Yet her blood "sings" to him as the most enticing form of forbidden fruit he has ever had to resist. The temptation of Bella's blood is a constant threat.

There is also the forbidden fruit of sex between humans and vampires. Edward's body calls to Bella just as surely as her blood sings for him. Everything about Edward entices Bella—his fragrance, his beauty, the velvety sound of his voice, his hypnotizing eyes. She longs to consummate their love. Yet there is mortal danger in doing so, because her fragile human body cannot withstand Edward's bone-crushing strength, and there is too much risk that sexual passion will cause Edward to lose control of his thirst for Bella's blood. They cannot have sex without violence. Throughout the novels the tension builds with Bella's longing for the forbidden fruit of Edward's body.

And because of Edward's moral commitments they cannot have sex outside of marriage. Both of their bodies are forbidden fruit until they are married, a boundary that Bella resents. She finally agrees to marriage at age eighteen so that she can have Edward, but he first has to agree to change her into a vampire as part of the deal. She wants Edward to change her so that she can be with him and his family forever. She wants immortality so that she will never lose Edward. For Edward this change is another kind of forbidden fruit, because for the rest of her immortal life Bella would suffer the pain of blood thirst. She would struggle against her own instincts to kill and devour humans. Worst of all in Edward's eyes, to change Bella to a vampire would mean condemning her to God's judgment against the damned. Bella would lose her chance at salvation.

The theme of forbidden fruit spills over into Bella's relationship with Jacob. As Bella leans on Jacob for friendship after Edward disappears in *New Moon*, Jacob falls in love with her. He knows that she is still in love with Edward, not with him. Yet he admits he is addicted to her, a burning thirst that remains with him even after Edward and Bella are married (*Breaking Dawn*, 197). He knows he should quit her, but he cannot. He understands that he cannot force her to love him, but he struggles against the urge to do just that. At one point he gives in to temptation, kissing Bella against her will (*Eclipse*, 330). Only after Jacob imprints on newborn Renesmee is he able to shake his obsession to have Bella.

Back to Eden

Having identified the many kinds of forbidden fruit in the Twilight saga, let's return to Eden to consider the original forbidden fruit. What is the nature of temptation in Eden? What are the thirsts? How do the characters handle it? Then we will be ready to identify and reflect on Meyer's interpretive use of the Genesis text. Finally, we will consider what the idea of forbidden fruit means for Christians.

Eden. When most Americans first encounter the story of Eden, we imagine a lush, tropical paradise, something exotic and far away. In *From Twilight to Breaking Dawn*, Sandra L. Gravett provides a wonderful analysis of Forks as a type of Eden, where the Genesis narrative plays out through Edward and Bella:

> Much like the biblical garden provides a setting for extraordinary events such as serpents speaking (Gen. 3:1–5) and deities walking in the cool of the day (Gen. 3:8), the primal wilderness of Forks, shrouded in fog and gloom, serves as the perfect setting for the mysteries of its many occupants. Meyer's garden conjures up creatures that could not exist in places like Phoenix with its bright sun and the strong overlay of civilization.[3]

As already noted, there are multiple thirsts involved in the temptation of Adam and Eve. The Bible tells the story with poetic wisdom:

> The LORD God took the man and put him in the garden of Eden to till it and keep it. And the LORD God commanded the man, "You may freely eat of every tree of the garden; but of the tree of the knowledge of good and evil you shall not eat, for in the day that you eat of it you shall die." (Gen. 2:15–17)

> Now the serpent was more crafty than any other wild animal that the LORD God had made. He said to the woman, "Did God say, 'You shall not eat from any tree in the garden'?" The woman said to the serpent, "We may eat of the fruit of the trees in the garden; but God said, 'You shall not eat of the fruit of the tree that is in the middle of the garden, nor shall you touch it, or you

shall die.'" But the serpent said to the woman, "You will not die; for God knows that when you eat of it your eyes will be opened, and you will be like God, knowing good and evil." So when the woman saw that the tree was good for food, and that it was a delight to the eyes, and that the tree was to be desired to make one wise, she took of its fruit and ate; and she also gave some to her husband, who was with her, and he ate. Then the eyes of both were opened, and they knew that they were naked; and they sewed fig leaves together and made loincloths for themselves. (Gen. 3:1–7)

Unlike its popular portrayal in everything from plumbing ads to book jackets for vampire stories, the forbidden fruit of Genesis is not an apple but the "fruit" of knowledge of good and evil. Clearly this is a symbolic use of the word "fruit." In ancient Hebrew thought, to "know" something is to participate in it. Eating the fruit of the forbidden tree therefore means participating in good *and evil*. Fruit is also the seed-bearing byproduct of a tree or plant, so we can think of this symbolic fruit in Genesis as the byproduct of experientially knowing both good and evil, something that passes the seed of the plant to the eater. God tells Adam and Eve that they may eat (participate in) all the many fruits of the garden, but not this one. God warns them that the day they eat the fruit (the seed-bearing byproduct of evil) they will die, a thing they cannot fathom in their state of unknowing.

Christians have interpreted the motivations of Adam and Eve in eating the fruit in several distinctly different ways. Ironically, Meyer seems to draw more from traditional, patriarchal Western interpretations than from her own Mormon theology. A quick tour through three major interpretations (Orthodox, Catholic/Protestant, and Mormon) will help us to see what Meyer is doing theologically with the Adam and Eve story.

Following the ancient theologian St. Irenaeus, Eastern Orthodox Christians have viewed Adam and Eve before the fall as immature humans, childlike in many ways. They are vulnerable, which means they can be deceived and hurt. God has not warned them to fear the serpent, only to avoid the forbidden fruit of the tree. They understand God's warning not to eat the fruit, but as already stated, they have no experiential knowledge of evil or its consequence of death.

When the serpent, whose origin is not explained by this text, tempts Adam and Eve, it is with the beauty and desirability of the fruit. Eve sees that the fruit is beautiful to look at and delicious to eat. How does she see that it is edible? Does the serpent take the first bite and offer some to the humans? The Bible does not say but with poetic nuance hints that Eve sees something that leads to this conclusion. The serpent tells them that the fruit will make them wise, just like the God they love. It is a good, normal, and healthy thing for children to want to be like their parents and for an immature Adam and Eve to want to be wise like the God who walks with them in the cool of the evening. The tempter plays on the normal, God-given thirsts in Adam and Eve for food, beauty, wisdom, and significance. It also tempts them in the thirst for community as Eve hands the fruit to Adam and they share the experience of a common meal with the serpent.

The Western (by which we mean Catholic and Protestant) interpretation of this passage is quite different, emphasizing the doctrine of original sin, a perspective that is absent in Eastern Orthodox or Mormon understandings. In the Western interpretation Eve persuades Adam to eat the fruit of sin, and it is an explicitly sexual invitation. She holds forth the juicy fruit with a coy smile, and poor Adam cannot resist. He is, after all, just a man. These interpretations are causally linked to women's sexuality, with Eve being cast as a precociously sexual being who tempts Adam to sin against God, thus damning the human race. The sexualized bias against women shows up, for example, in many artistic renderings of the fall, with the lascivious serpent woven around the tree, suggesting evil thoughts to the gullible woman.

Linked to this interpretation is the notion that original sin is rooted in prideful rebellion because Adam and Eve wanted to be like God. The assumption of course is that wanting to be like God means wanting to displace God, a defiant motive that is by no means clear in the text itself. The premier theologian of the Western church who promoted this view was St. Augustine, whose theology of sin included the notion that original sin is passed on physiologically from generation to generation through sexual intercourse. Since the seed of sin is carried through the seed of man, sex becomes a kind of necessary evil. We have to have sex to procreate, but there is that nasty original sin being passed on through the act. Many theologians today, myself included, have serious problems with this interpretation because of its misogynistic (i.e., woman-hating) view of women and its dismal view of human sexuality. There is also a substantial problem with its understanding of how people become sinful.

Mormon theology of what happened in Eden is quite different from these traditional, Western readings and from Orthodox theology. In the Mormon interpretation, Adam and Eve could not follow God's command to be fruitful and multiply unless they also broke God's command and "ate the fruit," which meant acquiring knowledge of good and evil. God gave them two conflicting commands. In order to have children, Adam and Eve would have to figuratively leave their immortal state of innocence as well as physically leave the abundant garden of Eden. Eve was heroic in that she was the first to realize she would have to give her life by eating the fruit so that the rest of the human race could be born. Eve chose to die so that generations of humanity might live.[4] In the Mormon version, Adam and Eve did not fall into "original sin." Their choice was not a failure but a gift to the future human race; it was a transgression, not a sin. Stephenie Meyer subtly (and probably unintentionally) perverts this classic Mormon theology in the Twilight novels. Unlike Eve, Bella wants to be immortal even if it means she can never have children. The Mormon Eve understands that immortality in a state of eternal childlessness is its own kind of living death.

These, then, are three historic ways of understanding the narrative of Genesis 3. But what does the biblical text actually say? And what is Meyer communicating about temptation, forbidden fruit, and sin through her use of the biblical text?

Some contemporary Bible commentators say that this story isn't about sin so much as it is symbolic of the transition from the innocence of childhood through puberty into adulthood with sexual awakening. After all, the man and woman realize they are naked after they eat the fruit, and they feel a need to cover themselves. In this interpretation their judgment of being banned from the garden is archetypal of the truth that none of us can return to our idyllic childhood. Adult life includes sex, childbirth, thorns, toil, and pain, and that's simply the way it is. The trouble with this "values free" interpretation is that it glosses over the annoying details of the story, with its talk of deception, choice, consequences, and shame. So we have to go back to the text itself and wrestle with that.

The Bible does not say that Eve seduced Adam, or that they wanted to dethrone God, or that Adam and Eve had sex and made God mad either because God hates sex or because Adam and Eve weren't married yet. These are the kinds of explanations that proliferate in Sunday school classes and sermons that don't look beyond the surface of the text. (Actually, if you take the story literally, who could have performed their wedding ceremony when they were the only two people on earth? There is also the problem that Eve was made out of Adam's rib, sharing his DNA, making her something like a sister. As you can see, too literal an interpretation of this story is riddled with problems.)

No, this is not a story about the sins of premarital sex or the inherent gullibility and deviousness of women. It is not a narrative that teaches us that sex and women are the root of all sin. Nor does it make sense that the story is a benign, artful way of talking about the transition from youth to adulthood when the text clearly talks about deception, sin, consequences, shame, and grace. What the Bible does say is that Adam was *with* Eve while the serpent tempted *them*, so Adam could hear and think about everything the serpent said. The text also insists that they were *deceived*. They were tricked, in other words, into thinking that the forbidden fruit might be a good thing, like all the other fruit in the garden. They were duped into believing they could be like God if they ate the fruit and that theirs was a good and holy thirst. And when they ate and their eyes were opened, the shame and alienation that resulted from having been deceived were comprehensive, reaching into their sexuality and dividing them from one another, God, and creation. We know this by the words of the text and the fact that the leaves of the fig tree are abrasive and painful. There was a self-punishing aspect to covering the most sensitive part of their bodies with something that felt like stinging nettles, a symbolic action that indicates shame and anxiety about their sexuality. Finally, the story ends with God's exchanging soft animal hides for the painful fig leaves, and even though the humans must now endure consequences of sin, they are sent forth with a promise of salvation. From the woman's offspring would come one who would strike the serpent's head. The story ends with grace.

What we have in this story is the template of how original wounds (rather than sin) lead to the bondage of sin, and what God does about that. The wounding of Adam and Eve by the serpent's deception precedes their act of eating. Genesis 2–3 is a narrative that shows the powerful sequence of events that lead us from innocence and vulnerability to deception and wounds, and then into the misery of sin. This story tells how temptation taps into God-given thirsts and how, as a consequence of eating forbidden fruit to satisfy our thirst, we become those who pass the fruit of sin on to others.[5] The core reality of all vampire stories (including Twilight) is that the eating of forbidden fruit leads to the replication of sin, the passing on of seed-bearing fruit to others. The vampire bites the human, who then becomes a vampire who bites more humans. All vampire stories are about forbidden fruit.

Meyer's Midrash

As we've seen, Stephenie Meyer begins *Twilight* with a quote from Genesis 2:17 about not eating from the tree of the knowledge of good and evil. She does this to let us know that we are about to read a story that draws from the Genesis narrative. And as we move into the saga, we discover that her view of Genesis is very much shaped by a Western reading, one that reinforces negative stereotypes of women, Eve in particular.

When Bella meets Edward in Biology, he treats her with disgust. Already her forbidden blood is "singing" to him, but Bella does not know this. As she ponders the possible reasons for his aversion, she says to herself, "He didn't know me from Eve" (*Twilight*, 24). This means that at a logical level she realizes that he doesn't know her, so his strange behavior couldn't be about her but is probably about something in him. Even so, she feels humiliated by his reaction. The irony in Bella's statement is that Eve is the progenitor of a new race of beings in the Bible and in this unfolding story. "Eve" means the mother of all the living, or life bearer. Bella is a type of Eve, whose blood "sings" to Edward as food and whose body calls to him for sex, tempting him toward the eventual coupling that will result in the birth of a half-human, half-vampire child.

Bella's attractiveness to Edward is cast in starkly wicked terms. Edward says Bella is like a "demon" from his "own personal hell," tempting him to ruin through her siren fragrance (*Twilight*, 269–70). She is the serpent and Eve all rolled into one. At one point Bella asks Edward, point blank, "Which is tempting you more, my blood or my body?" (*New Moon*, 52). She finds it exciting to tempt him. In both of these instances the Eve motif is misogynistic and patriarchal. It links Bella with the Eve of the Western tradition, and it links Edward with Adam as the one being seduced. This is especially true for readers who have been indoctrinated to a Western reading of Genesis. And in light of the pervasive presence of the Western reading in pop culture, this includes vast numbers of people who never go to church.

How does Meyer resolve the problem of forbidden fruit in Twilight? She does it by putting Edward in charge. Edward holds the reins in this morality play. Unlike Adam in the Bible, Edward exerts herculean spiritual strength in resisting Bella's sexual advances before marriage and in abstaining from the forbidden fruit of Bella's blood. He is only able to resist because of the depth of his love for her. He would rather die or give Bella up forever than see Bella lose her chance for salvation (*Eclipse*, 453). He says that he refuses to "damn her to an eternity of night" (*Twilight*, 476). This aspect of the story is both very beautiful and very harmful. It is beautiful because it demonstrates the power of love to overcome even the most severe temptation. It is dreadful because once again, the woman is the temptress and once again the man is the one who must resist her feminine wiles. And not only is the moral hero the male, he is a vampire—one of the living dead. In Meyer's imagined universe, even a blood-sucking, lust-inducing male vampire is morally superior to a woman.

Readers, are you angry yet? If you aren't it's probably because the whole thing is complicated. It would be easier to throw the book across the room if Edward's example of self-denying love wasn't so Christ-like. Despite all the problems of Edward's controlling and at times abusive traits, in his own way Edward practices the Greek theological word "*kenosis,*" which means "self-emptying." This word is found in one of the first worship songs ever written about Jesus. Scholars call it "the kenotic hymn," found in Philippians 2:6–11. Edward's behavior of self-denial for love's sake is a kind of lesser, vampiric version of verses 6–8, which say that Jesus, "who though he was in the form of God, did not regard equality with God as something to be exploited, but emptied himself, taking the form of a slave, being born in human likeness, and being found in human form, he humbled himself and became obedient to the point of death, even death on a cross." What I mean is that Edward, who looks human but is immortal, who could use his power over Bella to take whatever he wants, when he wants, actually divests himself of that power in order to protect her human life. He abstains from fulfilling normal, natural thirsts in order to promote the well-being of his beloved now and forever. Love alone can empower this kind of resistance to forbidden fruit.

To summarize, thus far in this chapter we have taken a closer look at thirst, which is bound to the essence of holiness and the essence of sin. We focused on temptation to eat the forbidden fruit, and we reflected on three very different interpretations of the original biblical story from which that image is drawn. Although there is much in Meyer's use of the Genesis narrative that is bad news for women, we also noted the Christ-like element of Edward's kenotic way. In the final section of this chapter we will think about the other side of thirst, which is the potential for thirst to lead us home to Love.

Eros and Ecstasy

When Bella touches Edward, her heart leaps with desire. This is more than a figure of speech. At the end of *Twilight,* when Edward kisses Bella in the hospital, the heart monitor stops, then lurches wildly (*Twilight,* 463–64). Bella is utterly given over to her longing for Edward, whose beauty is complete—body, mind, and soul (*Breaking Dawn,* 24). He has become her reason for existence. Edward feels the same about Bella. Aro, the Volturi leader, marvels at Edward's capacity to resist Bella's blood because it is so extraordinarily potent (*New Moon,* 471–72, 490). In his several thousand years of existence, Aro has never seen the strength of a love like Edward's.

And that is what gives this story lasting power. Despite all the disappointments of Edward's behavior and the gender issues in the Twilight saga, it is an enduring tale of true love, which is why it has been translated into dozens of languages around the world. It is a story of love prevailing against all odds and surviving the most difficult of tests, especially the test of forbidden fruit.

True love is about more than a thirst to *have* the beloved. It is more than a sexual infatuation. It is about the longing to *give* oneself to the beloved—to serve, to support, to bless and to honor even while yearning to be loved in return. This is why true love is never controlling, exploitive, or manipulative. The will to dominate is opposed to the giving practices of love.

There is a Greek word—*eros*—for the kind of love that I am talking about. Our English word, *erotic,* draws from the word *eros,* but in our exploitively sexualized culture we miss the deep spirituality of the original word. We tend to think of erotic love as an inherently selfish, get-what-I-want kind of sexy attraction. We use the word *erotic* to describe pornography, for example, which is rarely about honoring the other. It is safe to say that we have cheapened and abused this word to the point that it is almost impossible to speak of it without eliciting debased and exploitive connotations. It is common to hear pastors and church leaders talk about *agape,* the Greek word for unconditional love, but we never hear a peep about *eros.* Small wonder that most of us never knew what eros really is, or that it originates in God. (By the way, this is one of the reasons there are so many problems in the church with sexuality. Few Christians know how to think about it holistically, so we fear it and try to tame its fire.)

Many of the great saints, mystics, and theologians of the church teach us that eros is the energy of desire within the Trinity. It is a yearning toward union with the other, yet without diminishment or loss of either. (The threeness and the oneness don't cancel out, swallow, or suffocate each other.) There are hints of the yearning, orienting power of eros in Bella's reference to herself being a moon to Edward's planet (*Eclipse*, 68).

Eros is the creative dynamo of life. God has lovingly bestowed this life-giving energy on creation, leaving what St. Bonaventure called divine "footprints" everywhere. That is, in every aspect of creation there are signs of God's personality, including signs of eros. As Edward and Bella fall in love, their desire for one another saturates every aspect of their existence. Everything reminds them of each other. This element of the story reflects the intoxicating potency of eros and the way in which it is not limited to sexual activity but is woven throughout all aspects of life.

Wherever there is a pull toward union in the natural world, there are traces of divine eros. We find these echoes in phenomena such as photosynthesis, with leaves reaching toward the light, and in tides, with oceans responding to the gravitational pull of the moon. The interdependence of ecosystems reflects the energy of eros. Seasonal changes, the earth rotating on its axis, breath moving in and out of our lungs—all of this pulsing, dancing life bears the footprints of God. The pull toward union is intensely felt through sexual desire.

Part of humanity's being made in the image of God includes having eros at the core of our being. It is in all of us, woven into our bodies, minds, and spirits. Eros is playfully present in all forms of human creativity, whether art, music, horticulture, engineering, making soup, or writing a book about Twilight. Compassion, which is the medicinal, life-giving power to suffer with the other, is yet another expression of eros.

One of the most potent expressions of eros is when two people come to love each other deeply in body, mind, and spirit, and in a covenant of mutual, self-giving surrender to each other. This kind of union is what Edward and Bella long for, and the yearning for this union is the energy that drives the story from one novel to the next, beckoning readers on. Eros in this case is sexual, compassionate, playful, and creative. The act of conception is meant to come from this kind of powerful union, with the new life carrying DNA from father and mother without depleting or diminishing either parent. The twoness becomes threeness, and even more as additional family members are born. In Twilight the consummation of Edward and Bella's desire leads to the surprising pregnancy with Renesmee, who disarms everyone who meets her with her innate beauty and goodness. Eros leads to new life.

Eros (desire) leads also to action, reflected in another Greek word, *ecstasis*. The prefix *ec* means to go out, and *stasis* means static or unchanging. The English word is *ecstasy*. So *ecstasy* means to leave a static position and to go out or be carried beyond ourselves. Here, too, our sexualized culture has impoverished the fuller, spiritual meaning of this word. We tend to think of ecstasy as intense pleasure, especially erotic pleasure, not realizing that the original word refers to being called out of oneself by a power greater than ourselves. It can have sexual meanings, but it is much bigger than that. Edward's love for Bella is ecstatic in that it carries him beyond his own appetites and thirst for blood so that he protects Bella.

If you can bear with me for just one more theological word, it will help us to get our minds around the idea of eros and ecstasy originating in God and to see more clearly what that has to do with Edward and Bella. The Greek term is *perichoresis*, meaning "circle dance." You may recognize its two roots, *peri* (around), from which we derive our English word *perimeter*, and *choresis* (to dance), from which comes our word *choreograph*. Since antiquity, theologians in the Eastern Orthodox church have used the metaphor of a joyous circle dance to explain the mystery of God as loving and redeeming Trinity. God the Father, God the Son, and God the Holy Spirit are like a community of dancers in a joyous choreography of life. Eros is the desire to dance. Ecstasy is the actual dance. Eros in the Trinity is the desire that leads to all of God's creative, redeeming, and compassionate acts on our behalf, for we are God's beloved, the apple of God's eye. Ecstasy is the collaborative "going out of stasis" action of God the Father, God the Son, and God the Holy Spirit bringing about creation, salvation, healing, and the making of all things new.

True love, the kind that Edward and Bella share despite all the problems I have named, reflects this dance of the Trinity. In their mutual, self-giving love, in their willingness to suffer with and for one another, and in their creative outreach to the people (and werewolves and vampires) around them, Edward and Bella demonstrate some of the beautiful, God-given energy of eros and ecstasy. Edward's willingness to forego a relationship with Bella so that she might have a chance at eternal life reflects the self-emptying eros and ecstasy of Christ. Bella's willingness to give her life for Edward during the attack of the vampire newborns also images Christ's eros and ecstasy (*Eclipse*, 539).

To be human is to be made in the image of this circle-dancing, Three-in-One God. Deep within our thirsts, our natural and God-given desires for food, touch, belonging, and significance are footprints of the divine eros. Forbidden fruit is a temptation to satisfy these thirsts with ways, means, or times that seem delicious but will result in death, not life. The outcome of eating forbidden fruit is alienation, shame, and the dissemination of seeds of death to others.

In the next chapter we will think about the problem of death, specifically in Bella's life. If Bella is going to stay with Edward forever, she must undergo a conversion. But this, too, involves a kind of death. Vampire stories of all kinds, in addition to being tales of forbidden fruit, are also narratives of salvation. What does it mean to be converted, to experience salvation in Twilight? Who or what is the savior?

Chapter Five

Born Again

Vampire stories are all about forbidden fruit, which means they are about hunger, temptation, deceit, sin, and death. Twilight is thoroughly vampiric in this way. But as anyone who has read Genesis knows, sin doesn't have the last word. Love wins the day. The head of the serpent will be crushed. Salvation is on the way.

Stephenie Meyer does not disappoint in presenting the good news of salvation. The preface of the first novel opens with a teaser, our Bella staring into a sadistic vampire's face. She is preparing to die so that her mother might be saved. But what does salvation really mean in Twilight? What is one saved from—sin? What is one saved for—heaven? What is the process of conversion, and just who is the savior? Where does God fit in?

Conversion Begins with Sin

Let's begin with sin. No one in the Twilight saga talks about sin, but don't let that fool you. All the major characters have clear concepts of sin that are simply clothed in nonreligious language. Although they don't use the word "sin," I will use it in the discussion that follows, since our goal in this chapter is to look at sin, conversion, and salvation in Twilight.

The narrative universe of Twilight reflects the postmodern culture of most readers, in which there is no longer a monolithic religious metanarrative. That is, we have mostly given up in Western, pluralistic, globalized cultures on a single, authoritative religious story that everyone accepts about God, the meaning of life, the nature of sin, or salvation. As Dorothy suggested to Toto in *The Wizard of Oz*, we aren't in Kansas anymore.

The acceptance of multiple religious truths or systems as all having equal value is one of the signal features of postmodern culture. Many people now believe that truth is relative, not absolute, especially in regard to religious beliefs. In this climate many people no longer believe in sin. For them the notion of sin is relative, if it exists at all. Nearly all people, however, have a moral compass or conscience, with a sense of right and wrong, virtue and vice. (To lack some kind of conscience is to be, according to the *Diagnostic and Statistical Manual of Mental Disorders*, a sociopath.)

In the postmodern world of Twilight where no one talks about sin, there are several roughly developed clusters of spiritual beliefs, each having a moral compass. I hesitate to call them "theological systems" because none is detailed enough to warrant that label. Even so, enough material is given to clearly mark out three clusters of beliefs about sin, salvation, and conversion for Edward, Bella, and Carlisle.

Dave Roberts comments in his book *The Twilight Gospel* that "the moral centre of the story is found in the interplay between the beliefs of Edward and Carlisle," even though most of the story is told from Bella's point of view.[1] He makes his case based on the more explicitly religious dialogue between Edward and Carlisle. Here as elsewhere in his analysis, Roberts's focus on using the "correct" Christian religious narrative hinders his ability to see the gospel-oriented spiritual formation that unfolds beneath Bella's seemingly irreligious worldview. For the same reason Roberts is appallingly dismissive of the Quileute's Native American beliefs in the story, saying "for many Western readers the Native American myths are too fantastic to be anything other than a story."[2] Sadly, Roberts misses the point altogether on the way fantasy, myth, and folklore function to tell the truth. As Kurt Bruner notes in *The Twilight Phenomenon*, good fiction helps us to *connect* with reality, not escape it, with Twilight being a good example.[3] Bruner rightly explains that the spirituality of a story rests as much in the lens of the interpreter as in the religious assumptions the author has embedded in the tale.[4] To get at the spiritual meaning the reader first has to experience the story on its own terms. "We don't want to dissect a story before we've allowed ourselves to experience it," he says. "Fantasy tales are meals to be enjoyed, not homework to be endured."[5]

Whatever religious views Stephenie Meyer may or may not have intended in the story, Carlisle, Edward, and Bella are a moral triad, with each of them growing in their spirituality as the story unfolds and with each learning new depths of sacrificial and saving love from the other two. The story would not happen without Bella at the center.

The Volturi also have a set of ethical standards, but we will save that discussion for chapter 6. Part of the creative tension of this story is the conflict between these different clusters of beliefs. With that introduction, let's turn our attention to the permanently seventeen-year-old Edward, a one-time prodigal son who returned to a welcoming, grace-filled father and mother (*Twilight*, 342–43).

Overcoming: Salvation According to Edward

When Edward finally comes clean with Bella about his identity, he does everything in his power to scare her away. Though Sandra Gravett argues that Edward is trying to save his own soul, Edward does this for Bella's own good.[6] Edward lets Bella know that he has killed many times in the past and that he especially longs to kill her, since her blood is his own brand of heroin. But he also tells her with great sorrow that he doesn't want to be "a monster" (*Twilight*, 187). Edward believes that vampires are, in fact, monsters. They are inherently evil, their capacity for heaven having been destroyed when they left mortality behind (*New Moon*, 518). Though he is not entirely convinced about the existence of heaven, Edward does believe that there is a divine Creator and that the world could not have simply appeared without that designer's plan. Edward acknowledges that hell is a possibility, and he is almost certain that when vampires die, whatever comes next for them cannot be good. For vampires all salvific hope is lost. They either cease to exist, or they suffer eternal damnation. This is why Edward wants Bella to grow old and die as a human, so that she can have a shot at salvation or heaven or whatever comes next (*New Moon*, 518). But he is deeply conflicted about Bella because he wants her in every possible way. As long as she is human, she is at risk with him. When Edward realizes that he can no longer stay away from Bella, he says that since he is "going to hell anyway," he "might as well do it thoroughly" (*Twilight*, 87).

In Edward's schema, murder of humans is the Great Sin. Vampires are monsters precisely because they kill humans and drink their victims' blood.[7] Edward cannot imagine a universe of grace where a "monster" such as himself might find forgiveness and divine empowerment to become a new kind of person. Vampires are unforgiveable. Instead, he hopes that in his limited way he might do some good in the world by at least avoiding the sin of murder.

Yet his abhorrence of murder is not universal. Although Edward thinks that it is wrong to take a human life, he wants Bella to have an abortion when she becomes pregnant in *Breaking Dawn*. Edward is nearly crazed with grief when each day Bella moves closer to death, the fetus draining and battering her from within. He feels deep guilt for having gotten her pregnant, a consequence of their union that neither of them foresaw because the idea of vampires impregnating humans seemed to be an old folk tale.

Edward's aversion to murder does not at first extend to his own unborn daughter, whom he sees as an enemy because she is killing Bella. Edward (and Carlisle, surprisingly) depersonalizes the child by calling her "the fetus." Bella, however, resists all talk of an abortion because she has already completely bonded with her child. She is horrified that Edward and Carlisle could conceive of such a thing. Meanwhile the baby grows within Bella at a supernatural rate, breaking Bella's ribs in the process.

Edward's position completely changes when he begins to "hear" the thoughts of the fetus. As soon as he recognizes her intelligence and humanity, including her feelings of love for both her parents, Edward is head over heels. "The fetus" is now his daughter. She has thoughts and feelings; she can love; thus she is human. To harm the fetus would be to go against everything Edward believes. It would violate the one way he can experience a measure of salvation in this life: by protecting the sanctity of human life. The fetus is human; therefore it is sacred. To sin is to violate something holy.

Edward is also old school when it comes to sexuality. Sex outside of marriage is unacceptable to him, as is sex without genuine love. While sexual sin is not nearly as damaging as murder, it is nonetheless a sin in Edward's moral universe. Edward, a virgin, tells Bella early in their romance that he thinks sex between them is impossible because it could kill her. As the conversation progresses, he asks whether Bella has ever been with anyone. Flustered, Bella responds, "Of course not . . . I told you I've never felt like this about anyone before, not even close." Edward responds, "I know love and lust don't always keep the same company" (*Twilight*, 310–11). No matter how aroused he becomes, Edward refuses to let Bella take her clothes off or push their relationship beyond kissing until they are married (*Eclipse*, 450).

To summarize, sin for Edward mostly consists of murder and fornication. Sin is not about a broken relationship with God particularly, nor is it contextualized in a specific religious tradition. It is not as Augustine and Martin Luther described—an orientation in which the soul is curved in on itself. Sin for Edward is about specific wrong actions involving murder and sex.

Part of the reason for such simplistic notions of sin is that Edward is essentially agnostic, which means "without knowledge" about God. Despite his agnosticism, though, Edward describes a conversion experience that changed his life. He tells Bella that his transformation took place a few years after he became a vampire.

Carlisle, who first created Edward, had taught Edward from the beginning that it is wrong to take a human life, but like many readers of the Twilight series, Edward experienced adolescent rebellion. He turned away from Carlisle for some time, feeding on human blood. Even though he only killed "bad" people, he grew increasingly depressed, loathing himself for what he had become. He came to understand that human life is precious, even that of sinners. Edward began to label himself a monster (*Twilight*, 342–43). When he could no longer endure the hateful self he had become, he returned to Carlisle and Esme, who received him with open arms. With Carlisle's help he converted back to the family's "vegetarian" ways.

Conversion for Edward, then, means overcoming his normal, "sinful" instincts to hunt humans. It means denying his thirst, struggling against nature, becoming more than (or less than) a vampire. This is a painful, ongoing process, not an instantaneous event, and it will never be completely finished in this life.

Edward's concept of eschatology (final things such as death, judgment, heaven, and hell) does not include much talk about salvation, other than the few times he says he doesn't want to ruin Bella's chance for heaven. But if he were to explain salvation, he would likely frame it in terms of choosing to protect human life here and now, in this world, because no one really knows what, if anything, happens after death. He would perhaps say he is being saved from himself by becoming more than himself. Salvation for Edward is a matter of moral choices on his part, with the encouragement of his "vegetarian" family and a generous dose of self-will. Several of these elements are consistent with Meyer's LDS theology. The struggle to overcome one's natural existence ("the natural man") is found in the book of Mosiah (3:19) in the Book of Mormon, which Meyer has stated is her favorite book.

God doesn't really fit into Edward's picture except as a question mark in the margins. The only grace in Edward's version of salvation is that which he shows to humans who would otherwise be his prey. He "saves" others from himself, especially Bella. Edward therefore is simultaneously a sinner in need of salvation, a sinner who is saved from himself, and the savior who saves others from himself. There is no need for God because pragmatically speaking Edward is his own god. But he is not the only savior in his world; Edward was first saved by Carlisle, and later on in significant ways by Bella.

Carlisle and the Great Sin of Exclusion

For Carlisle the real God is very important. Ironically, the Great Sin in Carlisle's theological world is one that is regularly perpetuated by Christians: the sin of judgment leading to exclusion. It is this sin committed by his clergyman father that resulted in Carlisle's becoming a vampire in the first place and then his growing into the kind of vampire the world has never seen—a good one. Carlisle's understanding of sin, conversion, and salvation conveys Meyer's most biting social critique against Christianity.

Carlisle was born in the seventeenth century, the son of a harsh, judgmental Anglican pastor. The large, hand-carved cross that adorns the Cullens' living room wall is an heirloom made long ago by Rev. Cullen. It once hung above his pulpit. Like many other Christian leaders in his day, Rev. Cullen feared and hated witches, werewolves, and vampires. He not only participated in the judgments and executions of many innocent people accused of witchcraft; he led these pogroms. Carlisle recalls with horror the death of those hapless souls who were burned at the stake (*Twilight*, 330–41; *New Moon*, 34–38).

Against the young man's will, Carlisle's father put him in charge of hunting expeditions against werewolves and vampires. Though most of these hunts focused on humans who had the ill fortune of being misjudged as monsters by the church, one night Carlisle's hunting party stumbled onto a real coven of vampires. In the fight that ensued Carlisle was bitten. He hid behind some debris, miraculously escaping the vampires, then after a few agonizing days emerged as a vampire. By allowing judgmentalism and hatred to drive his life, Carlisle's father drove his son to become part of the hated "other." (There is a profound truth for parents to ponder in this.)

Over time, Carlisle discovered that he could survive on animal blood and did not have to be a monster (*Twilight*, 337, 339–40). He had always had an aversion to killing humans, but it took two hundred years for him to perfect his resistance to the smell of human blood. Empowered by his ability, Carlisle decided to become a doctor so that he could devote himself to saving human life. This work as a healer brought peace to his troubled soul (*Twilight*, 339–40).

While cleansing a wound on Bella's arm in *New Moon*, Carlisle tells her some of this story. Bella is surprised by Carlisle's religious faith. He says that never in his nearly four hundred years has he doubted the existence of God, although like Edward, he is not sure of who or what God is. Carlisle says that even his own reflection in the mirror—a daily sign of monstrous evil in the world—does not make him doubt (*New Moon*, 36). But, he adds, he has never agreed with his father's type of Christian faith, with its harsh worldview and violent repression of those who are outside the church's norm.

Carlisle tells Bella that even though most people think vampires are damned, he hopes God will give them credit for trying to be good. He hopes for mercy and forgiveness, in other words, for himself and his family and any other vampires who make an effort to become agents of life instead of death. (Carlisle actually evangelizes other vampires to his peaceful way of life whenever he can. He helped the Denali coven to become a vegetarian family, for example.) Bella agrees with Carlisle that even God should be impressed by Edward's valiance. The only kind of heaven Bella can imagine is one that includes Edward (*New Moon*, 37). Carlisle responds that she is the first one ever to agree with him that a vampire could possibly go to heaven.

For Carlisle, then, the Great Sin is judgment and exclusion of "the other," whether that other is a vampire, a werewolf, a human, or any other sentient creature. In this way he resonates with theologian Miroslav Volf, who articulates the same theology in his award-winning book *Exclusion and Embrace*.[8] The most extreme form of the Great Sin of course is violence against the other, including murder. Carlisle is a pacifist until pressed to the absolute extreme; he does fight against Victoria's army at the end of *Eclipse*, for example, but when he sees the opportunity to persuade the newborn Bree Tanner to join their vegetarian ranks instead of killing her, this is the course of action he tries. If at all possible he eschews violence even against sadistic vampires like Victoria, James, and Laurent.

But Carlisle's perspective goes beyond Edward's. It's not enough merely to refrain from evil, as Edward does. In addition to abstaining from doing evil, Carlisle's salvation from the torment of being a monster includes doing good—becoming a healer in the world. He is like John Wesley, the founder of Methodism, in this way. Wesley's first two rules for spiritual life are to "first do no harm," and "do all the good you can."[9] As a doctor, Carlisle's exceptional intelligence, sense of smell, and other superhuman abilities are transformed from the tools of a killer into the medicine chest of a healer. Everything about Carlisle as a vampire is, in a sense, born again.

Though much of Carlisle's conversion and salvation are the result of his own efforts, he strongly believes in the existence of a good God, one from whom he hopes to receive an eternal reward. His hope of salvation extends beyond himself to any vampire who will engage the world as he has, especially the members of his own family. Thus he hopes for grace and mercy from God in addition to his own efforts toward salvation.

Edward describes Carlisle as the most humane, compassionate person in all of history, far more advanced than the rest of the Cullens or any other vampires (*Twilight*, 288). (Edward doesn't mention Jesus, whom Carlisle apparently surpasses with his goodness. Clearly they know about Jesus because of the cross on the wall and Carlisle's father.) This means that for Edward, Carlisle is a savior. In addition to saving humans from sickness in his work as a doctor, Carlisle saved Edward, Esme, Rosalie, and Emmett from death by turning them into vampires, thus creating a family for himself from those who were otherwise doomed. Sandra Gravett sees Carlisle functioning as God, creating people in his own image.[10]

One last irresistible little tidbit about Carlisle as savior: Toward the end of the first novel, Laurent, who travels with Victoria and James, comes to warn the Cullens that James is tracking Bella. Her life is in grave danger. With Edward, Jasper, and Emmett straining to tear Laurent's head off, Carlisle invites Laurent to stay and join them in their peaceful way of life. (Miroslav Volf would approve.) Laurent considers the possibility only for a moment, then declines. He says that he will go to Denali instead, to spend time with another coven. Carlisle extends a formal, pastoral benediction to

Laurent, the same words I have used hundreds of times when dismissing a congregation at the end of worship. "Go in peace," he says, knowing that nothing could be further from Laurent's mind (*Twilight*, 400). But in Carlisle's theological world, it is never too late for a bad vampire to repent.

To Die That Others Might Live:
Bella, Reconciliation, and Self-Sacrifice

Bella, Bella, Bella. What are we to think about the girl who keeps trying to die? Unlike the vampires for whom salvation in this life and possibly the next means rising above their incessant thirst for blood, Bella is determined to shed her blood for others so *they* can be saved. On the one hand, we could see this as a beautiful representation of Christ. On the other hand, it is the sort of thing feminists hate. Why does salvation for men mean a change of diet, but for a woman it means death? Is Bella required to die for others, or does she simply have, as they say, "issues"? There is more to sacrificial Bella than meets the eye. But first things first.

Unlike Edward and Carlisle, Bella has no religious beliefs whatsoever. She doesn't care about God, heaven, hell, or salvation as traditionally understood, mostly because of her defective parents. Her father is a nominal Lutheran whose real religion is fishing. Her mother drifts in and out of whatever trendy spirituality happens to be in vogue (*New Moon*, 36).

Bella is a hard-core agnostic who is respectful of Carlisle's faith but uninterested in sharing it. She doesn't give a fig that if she dies tonight she might not go to heaven. The fundamentalists would have a hard time if they knocked at her door. Bella says she doesn't care about her soul; Edward can have it (*New Moon*, 69). The thought that Edward or any other Cullen might spend eternity in hell for their crime of existence is an outrage to Bella. What kind of sick God would condemn her beautiful Edward?

Bella's offense at the God of damnation is tied to her moral compass. In Bella's spirituality the Great Sin is bigotry that leads to violence among sentient creatures. She lives in a crazy world where vampires hunt humans (who in some centuries hunt vampires). Werewolves and vampires are mortal enemies. Humans, especially religious types, burn people at the stake, lock up visionaries like Alice, launch wars, and do other evil acts for money, sex and power. Even within the vampire world there are turf wars, factions, and hostilities. Bella thinks all this strife is idiotic. Why can't everyone get along? It would make so much more sense. If Bella had a theme song it would be John Lennon's "Give Peace a Chance."[11]

So for Bella, salvation mostly circles around the idea of reconciliation. Note especially that rather than primarily being salvation for herself, she seeks salvation for her family and friends. In her mind salvation is not something that enables lost, broken, or monstrous creatures to reach heaven or avoid hell, nor does it have anything to do with God. Indeed salvation is a matter of being saved from the needless hostility and violence that are often caused by religion. The path of salvation is through loving relationships. Bella knows that it is hard to nurse prejudice against others with whom we eat, laugh, work, and play. So no matter where she goes or whom she's with (the one exception being other high school students), she takes a reconciling role, cultivating acceptance and friendship between "natural" enemies.

Bella's reconciling action is first seen in her relationship with Edward, her potential killer. In the face of his repeated assertions that he longs to kill her, Bella insists that he never will. She tells him that she is not afraid. Bella chooses vulnerability and trust, a posture that is due to her love for Edward. Empowered by love, Edward learns to control his thirst so that it is transformed into a passion for her safety. Thus because of Bella's love Edward's killer instinct is "born again." The two refer to themselves as the lion and the lamb, fallen in love (*Twilight*, 274), recalling the reconciliation images of Isaiah 11:6 and 65:25, in which a predator and its prey lie down together in peace.[12]

As the Twilight story unfolds, Bella learns of mutual revulsion between the Quileutes and the Cullens, an aversion borne of generations of enmity between vampires and werewolves. Because of Bella's friendship with Jacob she longs to see this bigotry dispelled. She knows that the Cullens are friends of humans, every bit as committed as the Quileutes to protecting people from bad vampires. But Jacob refuses to fully believe it. Like all other Quileute werewolves, it is his job to destroy vampires. If one should cross over onto Quileute land, it is the werewolves' sacred duty to kill it, even if "the leech" is a Cullen. Racist slurs go back and forth between the two, with the Quileutes calling the Cullens "leeches" and "bloodsuckers." The Cullens (except Carlisle and Esme) are just as rude, contemptuously referring to Jacob and his pack mates as "dogs." Both the Cullens and the Quileutes complain about the stench of the other race.

It is only when Victoria, James, and Laurent launch a campaign of destruction in Seattle and Port Angeles that the Quileutes and the Cullens overcome their hostility to cooperate for the common good. This turn of events happens directly because of Bella's relationship with both sides. By the end of the fourth novel Jacob and Edward have become close friends, an extraordinary outcome that could never have happened without Bella's reconciling presence.

Part of what brings these two factions together is Renesmee, the half-vampire, half-human daughter of Edward and Bella. Renesmee is in many ways "reconciliation incarnate," the offspring of an impossibly peaceful relationship between a human and vampire. Her very name reflects this union, a combination of her vampire grandmother's name, Esme, and her human grandmother's name, Renee. The cherubic Renesmee has the supernatural strength and power that go with being part vampire, but her bite is without venom. The capstone feature of Renesmee as reconciliation personified is that she is the one on whom Jacob, the werewolf, imprints. Forever afterward werewolves and vampires will be bound to see one another as kin because of this singular relationship. Like Bella's "interracial" marriage to Edward, Renesmee and Jacob model the peaceable kingdom.

Facilitating reconciliation between enemies, then, is a major part of what salvation means for Bella. Another element of equal importance, however, drives feminists to weeping and gnashing of teeth: Bella is willing to die sacrificially for her loved ones in order to save them, making her one of the premier saviors of the saga. The reason this bothers many feminists is that any blood sacrifice is a problem, but female sacrifice most of all. Women have suffered too much abuse already.

The reader gets a sneak preview of Bella as Christ figure from the preface of *Twilight,* which foreshadows the climax of the first novel. For Bible readers, it is significant that this clue comes immediately after the Genesis quote about forbidden fruit. It is a hint about what's coming next: "Where sin abounds, grace abounds much more" (Rom. 5:20, paraphrase). A savior is in the works. The head of the serpent will be crushed.

The second clue comes from a line just a few pages later (*Twilight,* 5). Bella says she is leaving the light (sunny Phoenix) to venture into the dark (rainy Forks). It is a signal that Bella will be like Christ, descending from the light of heaven to the gloom of sinful earth, to bring salvation to many who walk in darkness.

The first time Bella prepares to sacrifice herself is shortly after encountering Victoria, James, and Laurent, the bad vampires who crash the Cullen family baseball game. James decides to stalk Bella, as much for sport as for a meal. His intentions become clear within hours of the spoiled game. To enhance the thrill of the chase James creates an elaborate ruse to make Bella think he is holding her mother captive in Phoenix. He uses this deceit to lure Bella back to her childhood dance studio. Bella falls for the trick, escaping her protectors, Alice and Jasper, and going alone to the studio. Once inside she realizes that she has been duped. As James moves in for the kill Bella ponders, "Surely it was a good way to die, in the place of someone else, someone I loved. Noble, even. That ought to count for something" (*Twilight,* 1).[13]

Happily, Edward and the other Cullens arrive just in time, saving Bella's life and annihilating James. But Bella's will to die for others isn't over. When Victoria creates an army of newborn vampires to attack the Cullens and avenge James, our heroine devises another sacrificial plan. It comes to her in dreams after she hears the Quileute legend about the Third Wife and the Cold Woman, a tale already noted in chapter 3 (*Eclipse,* 260).

When Victoria and the army of newborns advance on the Cullens and Quileutes, Edward takes Bella to a remote meadow to hide her from Victoria. One of the werewolves, Seth, comes to provide additional protection. But the raging Victoria and her new partner, Riley, track them to their hiding place. As Edward, Victoria, Riley, and Seth are locked in battle, Bella mistakenly thinks Edward and Seth are about to lose. She decides that to protect Edward she must do what the Third Wife did. She grabs a shard of rock to slash herself, much to Victoria's amazement. Edward wastes no time, seizing the opportunity. Within moments the fight is over. Victoria is dead at last (*Eclipse*, 550–53). It is a salvific attempt on Bella's part but, as it turns out, utterly needless. Edward and Seth already had the advantage and would have won no matter what—Bella has been foiled in another attempt at sacrifice.

Bella is Born Again

Wondrously, the day finally comes when Bella really does save all her loved ones. It happens after her "conversion." When Bella undergoes transformation into a vampire, she is in many ways "born again." Her new life as an immortal gives her the freedom and power that she needs to truly protect her family and friends.

As noted in earlier chapters, when Bella marries Edward she is still a human. She becomes pregnant on their wedding night, and the rapidly growing fetus begins to kill Bella, battering her and draining her of life. Bella refuses to have an abortion, but through an intervention by Carlisle discovers that if she drinks human blood her condition improves. Suddenly, just a few weeks into the pregnancy, her body already swollen to full term, Bella begins to hemorrhage. The placenta has separated from her womb. With her life quickly ebbing away, only one thing can "heal" her. The baby must be delivered immediately, and Bella must become immortal.

Edward frantically takes a syringe filled with venom and shoots it directly into Bella's heart. Then he and Carlisle tear the baby free from its nearly granite-hard amniotic sac. Bella's conversion from human to vampire begins. It is a three-day process that feels something like being burned alive (*Eclipse*, 74; *Breaking Dawn*, 354, 380). Throughout this time Bella is conscious of the torment, longing for death, unable to find relief. The venom slowly burns her human frailties away, beginning with her heart and slowly spreading out to her limbs. It is a three-day descent into hell, a journey that parallels Christ's descent into hell according to traditional understandings of 1 Peter 3:18–19, and according to the Apostles' Creed.[14] Bella's body is paralyzed, and she cannot communicate with her loved ones. She has to wait for the full three days to take their course.

On the third day, like Jesus, Bella rises from the dead, stunning in her transformation. To the astonishment of the Cullens, new-born Bella has self-control over human blood that took Carlisle centuries to perfect. Whereas newborn vampires normally go wild with thirst, killing every human in sight, Bella can exercise restraint immediately. Unlike her former human self, the new Bella is godlike in her gifts and graces. She can run, jump, fight, hiss, and beat Emmett Cullen in arm wrestling. She is in every way more than a match for Edward, a change we will explore in greater detail in a later chapter.

Best of all in regard to our topic of salvation, born-again Bella still has her ability to resist mind reading; only now it has become a gift she can use for the common good. She has become what in vampire parlance is called "a shield," one of the most powerful forms of supernatural vampire abilities. This means that she can create an impenetrable force field around herself and others so that the fearsome mental attacks of the Volturi (who can telepathically cause pain, blindness, or confusion) can't get through.

As the novels build to a grand finale of gore and mayhem with the Volturi against the Cullens and their friends, Bella's gift as a shield is what saves the day. She is finally able to protect all her loved ones and see her dream of reconciliation come to full bloom (*Breaking Dawn*, 745). She becomes a savior through finally shedding her own blood (for her unborn child), then undergoing a grue-some three-day conversion that includes horrific, hellish suffering.

The Three Saviors Rolled into One

What we have here, then, is a trinity of saviors who are all quite limited in their "theologies of sin" and in what each one does that is salvific. But when you combine them into one, they collectively represent at least part of what sin, conversion, and salvation mean according to Jesus.

Sin

Edward sees sin as the taking of human life; Carlisle understands it as exclusion; and Bella identifies it as bigotry. Jesus, however, takes it to a much deeper level. All three of these Great Sins are evil in Jesus' eyes, and he exposes them in many Gospel parables. But Jesus goes to the taproot of sin, the basic posture in which we live our lives. Sin with a capital "S" is a surrendered and worshiping orientation toward anything that is not the real God.

False gods are called "idols" in the Bible. Children who go to Sunday school learn to connect the word *idol* with statues of golden calves in the Old Testament, but there are many, many idols in our lives, some of which seem deceptively good, even "Christian." The surprising list includes family, religious practices, church buildings, pastors, even the Bible itself. Only God is God. Idolatry of even good gifts such as these can breed all the forms of violence, exclusion, and hatred that mar our world. So in the gospel according to Jesus there is a difference between Sin (an orientation) and sin (an action). Holiness begins with orienting our lives toward God.

Jesus forgives our Sin, and through the indwelling Holy Spirit heals our spiritual wounds from the inside out so that we can have increasing power over sin. Because our orientation has changed to a Godward posture and because God actually lives within us now, we are increasingly able to say no to acts of sin and yes to acts of righteousness. (That is what sanctification means.) This beautiful theological truth is presented metaphorically when Edward puts the "healing venom" into Bella's heart, where it transforms her, burning away all that is of death, starting with her heart and moving outward to her limbs. Bella is not only raised to new life; she now has the power of self-control and profound gifts to use for the benefit of others.

Conversion

The Greek word *metanoia* is usually translated in English "to repent," a fundamental part of conversion. Most people don't know ancient Greek, so we can easily miss the action-packed meaning of this word. Metanoia is what happens when you think you are driving south on I-75 from Dallas to Houston and then suddenly realize that you are really heading north! It's important to get to Houston instead of Oklahoma, so you take the next exit, turn around, and go in the right direction. You metanoia. That is part of what Jesus means by conversion. It is the act of turning around and going in the right direction, toward God. There is a first time you willingly and intentionally do this, but metanoia is not a one-time event. We have to keep making this choice every time we find ourselves nosing back toward Oklahoma. (Note to readers from Oklahoma: Don't take this illustration personally.)

There is much more to conversion than repentance. Like Bella, we truly have to undergo rebirth. Human choice is not enough. Will power is not enough. Metanoia is the part that we do to cooperate with God. The part that we cannot do, that only God can do for us, is to breathe into us the very nature of God so that we are *able* to cooperate. God imparts to us, if we are willing to receive it, the very power that raised Jesus from the dead. It is the astonishing energy of pure love that triumphs over all death, sin, hell, and damnation. Nothing is more powerful than that.

This is why Jesus used the image of being "born again" when talking to the religious leader Nicodemus in John 3. It is as if we are being given new spiritual DNA. Exactly how this happens is a mystery as invisible yet palpable as the wind. When Jesus is preparing for his own death and three days in the tomb (again, remember Bella's three days), he tells his friends that after these things happen they should wait in Jerusalem until they receive the Holy Spirit. After that they will have power to be witnesses in rapidly expanding circles of Jerusalem, Judea, Samaria, and the uttermost parts of the earth. Conversion is complete when the new Christians are willing to bear witness to others about the new life in Christ.

In *Breaking Dawn* the Cullens send an urgent plea to vampire friends and acquaintances from around the world to come and bear witness to the new life that is Renesmee. The witnesses (the term Meyer uses) are to testify that Renesmee is a new creation, a hybrid human-vampire, and is not a forbidden immortal child (*Breaking Dawn*, 550–51). These witnesses must be willing to risk their lives to speak the truth to the Volturi, knowing the Volturi will oppose them.

The phrase "bearing witness" has religious overtones, requiring the witnesses to place communal well-being above their own individual safety. When the witnesses arrive, Edward briefs them on the challenge that lies ahead (*Breaking Dawn*, 590–93). The entire Volturi guard, the wives, and their entourage will descend upon Forks because of a false report that the Cullens have created an immortal child. Unless the truth can be told in a way that no one can refute, great evil will befall the Cullens. The Volturi will destroy them. Though Carlisle is pacifistic and insists that violence will not be necessary, the witnesses decide to prepare to fight, to defend their freedom and the truth (*Breaking Dawn*, 656–61).

The Volturi, the reader learns gradually, are only using the "forbidden child" issue as a cover for their real goal: to acquire Alice and Edward for their guard and to wipe out the Cullen family, which they regard as a competing coven (*Breaking Dawn*, 682). Like King Herod, who ordered the murder of all male children ages two and under in order to kill the Christ child (Matt.2:16), the Volturi are willing to engage in atrocities in order to protect their power. Bearing witness against them is a courageous political act of resistance. It may cost some of the witnesses their lives.

The word "witness" in Greek is *marturia*, from which we get our English word "martyr." To be a witness is to spend one's life in the redemptive mission of God, speaking the truth about new life in Christ and resisting oppression in solidarity with those who are oppressed. Jesus says that the Holy Spirit will give his friends so much power that they will have the same kind of love and perseverance that Jesus has in the face of opposition. They will gladly spend their lives for the love of God in this world. That is what happens at Pentecost in Acts 2: the Spirit comes; the people are ablaze with divine joy; and they can't keep the good news to themselves. They become witnesses. Pretty soon they are living in countercultural ways, and the combination of what they say and how they live creates a tremendous thirst in their neighbors. Because of their witness, more people come to know the living Christ. Conversion is complete when it is passed on to others through bearing witness.

Salvation

When we bring together the salvific works of our three characters from Twilight, we see some of the same outcomes Jesus accomplished.

First, there is the sanctity of life. Human life is sacred because humans are made in the image of God (Gen. 1:27). The reason Jesus came into the world, God incarnate, is because human life is too precious to consign to destruction. It is God's desire for every human to experience fullness of life, to be uncursed from all the forms of alienation and violence that plague human existence in a broken world. No price is too great for the Three-in-One to pay because God so greatly values human life.

Just as Carlisle sees the Great Sin as exclusion, Jesus' love is inclusive. It reaches beyond the boundaries of his own race, nationality, and religion of Judaism to embrace the entire world. The Good News of salvation is for all people, John's Gospel proclaims:

> For God so loved the world that he gave his only Son, so that everyone who believes in him may not perish but have eternal life.
>
> Indeed, God did not send the Son into the world to condemn the world, but in order that the world might be saved through him. (John 3:16–17)

The Gospel of Luke abounds with stories and images of Jesus' inclusive love. In a culture where women were marginalized, Luke tells us that women were among Jesus' most faithful disciples, financing his missionary trips with their own resources while traveling with him and the male disciples (Luke 8:1). In Luke we find the story of the Good Samaritan, where a hated Samaritan is the one who models divine love. Luke also brings us the story of the Prodigal Son, one of the most beloved narratives of inclusion in the Bible, a story that resonates with Edward in his own life.

At Pentecost when Jesus sends the Holy Spirit, all barriers are broken between gender, race, nationality, culture, and class. Just as Bella brings together vampires, humans, and werewolves, Jesus brings together people who have been divided by sinful walls of judgment and exclusion. Women and men from every station in life are touched by the fiery love of God, so much so that they are able to go out into the street and relate to people from other cultures, languages, and economic strata. The gospel of Jesus is a gospel of inclusion.

As you can see, Bella's reconciling work is entirely consistent with the gospel of Jesus. Indeed, to be a Christian is to become an "ambassador of reconciliation," according to the apostle Paul (2 Cor. 5:18). As St. Francis of Assisi says in his beautiful prayer, to be a Christian is to ask God to "make me an instrument of your peace."

The wondrous irony of this story is something Jesus himself must love. The saviors are vampires (Samaritans . . . Gentiles . . . women), the creatures voted least likely to ever get to heaven. These damned monsters are able to save others because they surrender to the power of love. The three unlikely saviors of Twilight—Edward, Carlisle, and Bella—are able to create a community of witnesses from a motley group of vampires and werewolves who never could have been a community before Bella's coming. Through reconciliation, trust, and love, the witnesses have what it takes to stand against the Volturi for the good of all. The creatures most in need of saving in this story are the humans, the majority of whom do not even know that vampires exist. But the good vampires save them anyway. And that, my friends, is the meaning of grace.

Chapter Six

Golden Eyes and Granite Flesh
The Meaning of Salvation

For the first three-and-a-half novels of the Twilight series, Bella longs to become a vampire. She wants to stay young forever with Edward. She yearns to be part of the Good Family, the Cullens. And she craves freedom from the clumsiness, weakness, and inadequacy that mark her life. Bella would love to be fearless, bold, graceful, strong, and invincible. She dreams of becoming Edward's equal in every way.

Despite all these longings and the ways that she imagined what it would be like, when Bella rises from the hell of her conversion, she is shocked at what she has become. Bella moves with the speed of thought and can see colors, hear sounds, and taste the air in ways that were impossible before (*Breaking Dawn*, 392 ff.). Ravishingly beautiful, her voice sounds like bells. She had known that she would get a new body like other vampires, one that was irresistibly attractive, but she had not been capable of imagining the new sensations she would experience.

To her amazement Bella is more sexual than ever. Before the venom burned away her mortality, Bella thought that she would have to give up the intoxication of arousal she felt for Edward (*Breaking Dawn*, 392). Bella believed that blood thirst would trump every other feeling, a frightening promise that Rosalie made to her in the movie *Eclipse*. Bella imagined it would take a long time to adjust to her resurrected form, that she would have to learn a new way of feeling sexual love. In anxious moments Bella even fretted that she might not be desirable to Edward once she was a vampire because she would no longer bear the fragrance of blood. But the instant that Edward curves his hand around her newborn face, she feels desire envelop her body (*Breaking Dawn*, 392). Edward responds to her arousal in kind.

Bella has risen from the dead to reconnect with her immortal husband, so that together they can enjoy an eternity of sexual bliss and parenthood. Insatiable, Bella and Edward spend many hours of every day engaged in wild vampire sex. At night while their cherubic daughter sleeps, the lusty couple finds joy in one another's arms till morning dawns. They never tire of sex or each other because they are vampires in love. While all the other features of her resurrection matter, the centerpiece of Bella's immortality is Edward.

Meyer's Mormon background is apparent here. The belief that the best outcome of salvation—marriage in the Celestial Kingdom—includes an eternity of spiritual procreation is unique to Mormon Christians. Catholic, Orthodox, and Protestant Christians do not believe that people have eternal marriages or that they can procreate in the hereafter. They base their position on Jesus' statement that there is no marriage in the resurrection.

Jesus only speaks of the topic once, when the Sadducees, who do not believe in a resurrection, try to test Jesus by asking him which husband a woman will be married to in heaven if she has had several husbands on earth. Jesus reprimands them for their ignorance of the Scriptures and of the power of God, then says the woman will not be married to anyone: "For in the resurrection they neither marry nor are given in marriage, but are like angels in heaven" (Matt. 22:30).

Although Bella's immortal libido does not find a parallel in Catholic, Orthodox, or Protestant beliefs about the resurrection, the amazing power and glory of her new body is consistent with most Christian traditions. Just as Bella could not have imagined the sensations she would feel as a vampire, Paul the apostle wrote that no one in this life has ever seen or heard the wondrous things that God has prepared for God's resurrected people (1 Cor. 2:9).

When Bella and the others turn into vampires, they resemble their former, human selves but are astonishingly better. Charlie recognizes Bella when he sees her for the first time as a vampire, but he knows she has radically changed (*Breaking Dawn*, 506–7). Several times he asks, "Bella?" as if he can't quite believe his eyes. This is something like what the Bible says about the similarity and difference between our mortal and immortal bodies. Paul writes that our mortal bodies are like a dull seed, while our resurrected bodies are like the full-grown plant that emerges from the seed (1 Cor. 15:35–49). When our bodies die, they are "sown" in weakness, decay, and death, like seeds falling into the earth. The immortal body is raised in power. It is incorruptible, glorious, and spiritual (vv. 42–44). Yet it is physical, too, for it is like the resurrected body of Christ (v. 49), who ate food, touched people, and could appear and disappear through solid walls after he rose from the dead.

The theme of resurrection in Twilight indeed has strong parallels in Christian theology. Christians of all traditions believe that through Christ people can go to heaven after they die. This is a big part of what is meant by "salvation." But is salvation *only* about going to heaven? And does heaven begin only after we die? The gospel according to Twilight is a potent message of salvation that is both now and not yet. Heaven is a condition more than a place. Salvation is spiritual but not religious.

Salvation That Is Spiritual But Not Religious

A man whose wife was a member of my church once told me, "You people are a bunch of weaklings. You use religion as a crutch because you can't handle the fact that life sucks and the poor get screwed and in the end, nothing really matters." Mercy. I told him that even though he felt that way, he was welcome in our church. I couldn't help it. I'm an evangelist.

The thing is there are a lot of people like my friend's husband (who, by the way, came to his son's baptism despite all the things he said). Many people think Christians are escapists because they believe our whole plan of salvation is to endure this fallen world as best we can, putting our "hand in the hand of the man from

Galilee"¹ so that we can gain heaven and flee from hell. They think that we imagine salvation as having nothing to do with life in this world, that in fact salvation is mostly *opposed* to life in this world. Getting "saved" is a ticket to heaven, a "fire insurance policy" to keep us out of hell. Hollywood images of heaven usually show a boring place with clouds, harps, and angels.

Like my friend's husband, none of the three saviors of Twilight—Carlisle, Edward, or Bella—are connected to the church or any other form of organized religion. We saw in the last chapter that all three of them express doubt about traditional Christianity, especially in relation to beliefs about salvation, heaven, hell, and resurrection. None of them ever speaks of Jesus. Yet they follow disciplined, self-denying lifestyles in order to protect the lives of vulnerable humans. They have moral values. They love their neighbors. They are spiritual but not religious.

Carlisle, Edward, and Bella are the voice of an entire generation of twentysomethings who are offended by institutional religion. The "spiritual but not religious" generation loathes what they have heard the church say about sin and salvation because exclusion, shame, fear, and judgment have been at the center of their experience of those doctrines. According to a recent study, more than 80 percent of young adults in the United States today have negative views of Christians and the church. They believe that Christians are judgmental hypocrites who are out of touch, arrogant, homophobic, aligned with right-wing politics, and greedy.²

The Great Sins of Carlisle, Edward, and Bella are a mirror for Christians to take a good, long look at our own need for *metanoia*, or transformation. Too often throughout history the church has joined the "powers and principalities" (Eph. 6:12) of this world to perpetrate all three of the Great Sins, and to do so in the name of Christ. Christians have sanctioned the Crusades, slavery, the oppression of women, the Inquisition, genocide, and fear of homosexuals. These are just a few examples of ways that misinformed Christians have spread a "gospel" of violence, exclusion, and oppression. For victims of that kind of religion the good news of the gospel is bad news indeed. Jesus is not the problem. Christians are.

Stephenie Meyer wasn't the only creative force at the dawn of the twenty-first century to give life to this kind of critique of religion. Simultaneous with the phenomenon of Twilight was an explosion of movies that featured the three Great Sins as inherent to Christianity. These included *Lord Save Us from Your Followers* (2010), *The Invention of Lying* (2009), *Religulous* (2008), *Jesus Camp* (2006), and *Saved* (2004).[3] Some of these films presented Christians as anti-intellectual, exploitive, shaming fanatics who were out of touch with the beauty and pain of the real world. Although there are exceptions, popular films and television shows (particularly *South Park*) rarely show Christians in a flattering light unless they are highlighting an exceptional figure like Mother Teresa.

We will look more closely at Christians' need for reform in the next chapter. For now we should simply note that each of these negative Hollywood stereotypes is based on the assumptions that Christians think salvation is only about the future and not about now, that salvation is only for the few and not the many, and that salvation has more to do with getting ready for a vague heaven someday than with healing a broken world here and now. These are also the tacit assumptions that Twilight makes about the church. So for Carlisle, Edward, and Bella salvation has nothing to do with religion. It has to do with relationships of love, respect, and trust.

Heaven or Hell

When Edward speaks of heaven and hell, he is uncertain what they are and even whether they exist. For example, in *Eclipse* Edward tells Bella that he wants her to have a shot at heaven, or "whatever there is after this life" (453). The thought that Bella might lose her chance to go to heaven if she becomes a vampire torments him (*New Moon,* 518). He believes that if there is a hell, it will be his fate to go there because he has murdered people (*Twilight,* 87). Edward is convinced that vampires' souls are already destroyed and cannot be saved (*New Moon,* 37).

Beyond Edward's convictions that if there is a hell, he will go there, hell is scarcely mentioned in the books. Carlisle and Bella object to Edward's fatalism about his own soul being damned. They cannot imagine a heaven without Edward. When Bella asks Carlisle if the hell question is the reason Edward resists changing her to a vampire, Carlisle says it is true, but he disagrees with Edward's refusal to hope for eternal salvation: "I look at my . . . *son.* His strength, his goodness, the brightness that shines out of him—and it only fuels that hope, that faith, more than ever. How could there not be more for one such as Edward?" (*New Moon*, 37).

Although they do not discuss spiritual issues with a religious leader, Carlisle, Edward, and Bella ask questions of one another about these matters, have long conversations about what they wonder, and make decisions based on what they hope will be a fair and just outcome in the afterlife. Eschatology (the theological name for doctrines of heaven, hell, and the final judgment) is the least of Carlisle's and Edward's worries most of the time, and it is never a concern for Bella. What the three really care about is how to live in this world.

This trio of permanently young adults represents an entire generation that is not motivated to right living by promises of salvation in heaven someday. Instead they are interested in a heaven of compassion, inclusion, and reconciliation, a heaven that begins now and hopefully continues after this life on earth. And that is exactly what Jesus means by "the kingdom of heaven."[4]

The Kingdom of Heaven Is Both/And

According to Jesus, the kingdom of heaven is something people can enter and receive in this life, a condition of God's presence and authority in which people can participate now as well as in the hereafter. Jesus uses creative images to explain the kingdom of heaven. It is a life of faith that grows like a grain of mustard seed that becomes a huge plant. The kingdom starts out in a hidden way for most believers, but like the yeast that a baker kneads into the dough, it eventually leavens every aspect of life. The kingdom is precious like a pearl, so it is worth searching for and worth all that we might sacrifice to find it. The kingdom of heaven is found in humble places, like a treasure hidden in a field. Jesus says it is like a banquet with lots of food and hospitality for the ones who need it most.

Entering the kingdom of heaven is something like Bella's becoming part of the Cullen family through her conversion into a vampire. Living in the kingdom is like Bella's adjustment to life as a vampire, an ongoing orientation that has both individual and communal dimensions as she embraces the Cullens' peaceable family values and vegetarian practices.

Jesus' parables and metaphors help us to know that the kingdom of heaven is about living in community with the God who is present, active, and loving in the world, here and now. This means that participation in the kingdom of heaven involves taking part in God's saving, healing love for all people and all of creation. Wherever there is sickness, pain, grief, violence, hunger, loneliness, and need, the kingdom of heaven is present and active through people who help. Some of those caring people are not even in the church because the kingdom of heaven is much larger than the church.

Carlisle, Edward, and Bella do not seem to have heard this version of the gospel. They feel an aversion to the Christian faith because they link it to a judgmental gospel of damnation, one that does not welcome "monsters" to heaven and that justifies witch hunts. As representatives of a generation of young adults who are offended by Christianity, these three raise important questions for the church. The doubts that Carlisle, Edward, and Bella express about heaven and hell are similar to those of people who reject organized religion.

Is Salvation a Matter of Destiny or Choice?

Along with these questions about heaven and salvation in Twilight, Stephenie Meyer brings in the Mormon belief that salvation is deeply rooted in human "agency," or free will. That is, people make moral choices that lead to salvation. People are capable of choosing the good. Meyer uses Alice's clairvoyance to express this core belief. When Alice gazes into the future, it is always conditional on the choices that people make (*Twilight*, 290). She tells Bella that even the smallest human choice can change the future, like the "butterfly effect" in chaos theory.[5] Although Alice sees Edward on a suicide mission to the Volturi, she acts quickly, taking Bella to intervene and stop Edward. It is not inevitable that Edward will die. Everything can change. People have real power in choice. Alice's gift functions not as an irrevocable prophecy of an unchangeable future but as a beacon for a fluid future, one that can be changed.

In Protestant theology there are at least two schools of thought that fit well with Twilight's flexible future, in which human choice makes a difference. These are process theology and open theism.[6] Both of these theologies propose that God has made humans as cocreators so that we can influence the unfolding of the future. The future is not predetermined. God has created humans to be partners, not puppets, in all of God's creative and saving work.

In Twilight, the universe is not predetermined. Salvation is a process shaped very much by human (and vampire) choice. The world of Stephenie Meyer's Twilight is one in which individuals exercise moral agency and take the consequences those decisions create. As we will see, salvation is a process of choice.

Golden Eyes: A Symbol of Salvation

Though it is easy to see parallels between Bella's transformation and Christian beliefs about a bodily resurrection from the dead, the more interesting and well-developed concept of salvation in this story has parallels with Jesus' teaching about living in heaven while on earth.

As already noted, each of the Cullens experienced a rebirth of sorts when they became vampires. Every one of them was at one time a limited mortal with all the frailties and vulnerabilities of human life. They were all bound for human death. Then they were born again through conversion and given a new life with "heal-ing" venom. The conversion for each of them took three days and worked from the inside out. As Alice tells Bella, the single most vivid memory every vampire has of human existence is the agony of conversion (*Twilight*, 414). Its fiery power cleansed them of their former weaknesses that led to death.

There is a way in which this transformation parallels Christian conversion, with the sacrament of baptism representing spiritual burial and resurrection to new life in Christ. John the Baptist told onlookers that he was baptizing with water but that the one coming after him would baptize with the Holy Spirit and with fire (Luke 3:16). The fire of the Spirit is the cleansing, renewing action of God, similar to the healing venom.

Because they have chosen to protect and not harm their human neighbors, by drinking animal instead of human blood, the Cullens have golden eyes. The vampires who drink human blood have crimson eyes. So the golden eyes are signifiers of a lifestyle of doing good and abstaining from evil. Kurt Bruner comments that the difference between a good and bad monster is "whether one destroys or protects human life and dignity."[7] Golden eyes are the sign of the good monster. Bruner also presents an imaginary con-versation between Edward and the apostle Paul over the struggle to do good while being drawn to evil. In that scenario Edward chides Paul for lacking will power while Paul via Scripture makes it clear that will power is never enough. Only the power of God can enable lasting change.[8]

The Cullens' golden eye color changes from day to day accord-ing to the degree of their thirst. Their temptation toward human blood never goes away. Sometimes the battle is fierce against the thirst. But they are a community of faith in this way, choosing to do the right thing together, giving one another support in this sacrificial choice. Salvation is worked out communally as well as individually, one decision at a time. The power that enables them to make the right decision is love. In Edward's case especially we can see how love transforms his intense thirst for Bella's blood into extraordinary passion for her protection.

We could say that golden eyes symbolize the ongoing process

of salvation (sanctification) in which Christians choose to do good and abstain from evil. Sanctification is the living out of salvation, the day-by-day embrace of the kingdom of heaven, something that is both individual and communal. The power that enables Christians to endure is the love of God given through the indwelling Holy Spirit. Galatians 5:16–17 tells Christians to walk in the Spirit and not in the old nature and says that the Spirit will give a new set of desires that are consistent with the love of God.

The community of faith or family of God functions as a support system and safety net so that all the members are more likely to grow in their ability to love. Just as Edward's thirst is transformed by a loving relationship with Bella, Christians' old self-seeking relational habits and hungers are transformed so that we increasingly regard all our human loves through the love of God, with God's interests for the others at heart.

Granite Flesh: A Symbol of Heaven on Earth

The Cullens are nearly invulnerable to the kinds of things that formerly would have done them in, such as being run over by a car or falling from a tree. They now have incredible strength and agility in the face of such dangers. This is because the Cullens have granite flesh. They have power to resist, to endure, to overcome.

When Jesus prepared his disciples for his impending death, he told them that the Holy Spirit would help them to endure trials, resist evil, and overcome temptation even though he wouldn't physically be with them any more: " 'I have told you all this so that you may have peace in me. Here on earth you will have many trials and sorrows. But take heart, because I have overcome the world' " (John 16:33, NLT).

The Lord's Prayer, which was Jesus' simple response when the disciples asked him to teach them to pray, includes the petition "Your will be done on earth as it is in heaven" (Matt. 6:10). At the heart of the Christian faith is the conviction that the kingdom of heaven is the condition of living in partnership with God in this life as well as in eternity. Christians believe that the Holy Spirit lives within people, empowering them to practice self-denial, to truly love others (even enemies), and to be part of God's work of salvation in this world.

So the golden eyes and granite flesh of the Cullens can remind us of the extraordinary, resurrection power of life in Christ, a power that is manifested in self-control and in serving the well-being of others, including the power to practice self-denial and sacrifice for the good of the other.

Special Gifts

Just as the Cullens illuminate the power of divine love to transform attitudes and hungers, they also help us to think about spiritual gifts that Christians receive from the Holy Spirit so that God's will can "be done on earth as it is in heaven." The gifts of the Holy Spirit are necessary so that people can live in the kingdom of heaven while on earth.

The idea that the Cullens' special gifts are good is unacceptable to Dave Roberts, who finds the powers "demonic" because they are not explicitly named as Christian gifts.[9] Roberts refers to the abilities as "mind gifts" that are in opposition to a Christian world-view, citing a story from Acts 16:16–19 in which Paul exorcises a clairvoyant slave girl.[10] Here as elsewhere, Roberts is unable to engage the mythic nature of the story. He is, as Tyler Chadwick notes, too literal, failing to grasp how stories of the supernatural help readers "withhold judgment as the story moves us to confront the many-faceted issues" of life in a morally complex world.[11]

In the narrative universe of Twilight the goodness of the gifts depends on how the gifts are used. For the Cullens, the gifts are undeniably good. Carlisle believes that when humans become vampires, they bring their strongest, best human traits into the immortal life, where for vampires they become special powers. (Those special powers, as we will see in the next chapter, are of great interest to the Volturi.)

Each of the Cullens has a unique gift. Carlisle is a healer with extraordinary compassion. He is able to empathize so deeply with human suffering that he overcomes his sensitivity to the smell of human blood. Esme is full of nurturing love for others, so much so that she is able to cook repulsive human food for Bella and share clothing with the foul-smelling werewolves. She overcomes her natural vampire repugnance because of her nurturing powers. Emmett has exceptional physical strength, which he uses for the common good. Rosalie has the power of tenacity, which in the end serves the community. Alice, who was a visionary as a human, has the gift of precognition, enabling her to see the future. She uses this gift to protect others from harm. Jasper had a charismatic personality in his human life but as a vampire has the power to infuse peace into others. Edward is able to read minds, a gift he uses to protect his family and vulnerable humans.

When Bella is a human, she has a deep desire to sacrifice herself to save others. As we've already seen, she sometimes chooses to demonstrate this gift in ways that are foolish and at times when her sacrifice is not needed. Yet as a vampire, her sacrificial, saving desire is transformed into unprecedented power to protect human life.

The rest of the Cullens are amazed by this. Never have they seen a newborn vampire exercise such self-control or empathy (*Breaking Dawn*, 466). Ordinarily a newborn goes on feeding frenzies. Jasper is particularly taken aback by Bella's self-control because after a century of effort he still struggles mightily against a thirst for human blood. Not only is Bella able to abstain easily from human blood, she becomes a shield for others. She is able to block manipulative, intrusive, or harmful mental powers of other vampires. Her new ability, honed with practice, gives her the strength to project her shield over an entire community.

When Bella extends her shield over the Cullens and their friends, a small plume of light appears over each one of them. The lights allow Bella to know which ones are protected within her shield (*Breaking Dawn*, 703). This is remarkably similar to what happens on the day of Pentecost. As the promised Holy Spirit is given, a plume of fire appears over the head of each believer. They are enlightened and empowered to go out into the world, with its diverse cultures and customs, and speak in new languages (Acts 2:1–13). They bear witness publicly and joyously in Jerusalem—on the same streets and to the same people who crucified Jesus just a few weeks back. The power of the Holy Spirit protects them from fear and enables them to engage in God's mission of salvation. The presence of the Holy Spirit in them breaks down sinful divisions of race, gender, ethnicity, and culture so that reconciliation is now possible. The Holy Spirit makes them into an inclusive community.

The gifts of the Holy Spirit are also given to the church, distributed according to the wisdom of the Spirit. One list of these gifts is found in 1 Corinthians 12, with some of the gifts similar to the special powers of the Cullens: wisdom, knowledge, faith, healing, prophecy, discernment of spirits, miracles, and the ability to speak in new languages. All of the spiritual gifts work together so that Christians are able to live in the kingdom of heaven now even though the fullness of heaven will not happen until death has been destroyed and Christ has made all things new (Rev. 21:5).

Salvation and the Natural World

In many Christian traditions, salvation, or the making of all things new, includes the healing of the natural world. Though Twilight offers few comments about saving creation, these remarks are significant.

When Edward explains the family's hunting practices to Bella, he tells her that they only hunt where it is environmentally responsible. They cull herds that are overpopulating an area, for example, or take out predators such as mountain lions that are becoming a danger to humans (*Twilight*, 215). At another time Edward tells Bella that "the wasting of finite resources is everyone's business" (*Twilight*, 83). This is a kingdom-of-heaven perspective, for it takes into account the interdependence of all living things. Salvation includes saving the earth from ecological destruction caused by sinful choice.

When Victoria, James, and Laurent go on a killing spree in Port Angeles, a hunting party from Forks goes out to kill the "big wolves." Werewolves have been sighted by a few people and are blamed for the deaths. The posse doesn't realize, of course, that these "animal attacks" are actually murders committed by vampires. As Charlie goes out on one of the hunts, Bella worries aloud that he might shoot one of the wolves. She knows that they are really young Quileute men in werewolf form. Charlie then calls Bella a "tree-hugger," a pejorative term used against conservationists and environmentalists (*New Moon*, 296–98). Charlie's use of this word contributes to his characterization as a defective, uninformed father. Edward Cullen would never use this kind of language, nor would Carlisle or Esme. The Cullens are a Good Family, ecologically informed and environmentally astute.

One of the most pointed comments about ecological care comes, strangely enough, from Aro, one of the Volturi leaders. In a climactic *Breaking Dawn* speech that brings to mind the work of eco-poet Wendell Berry, Aro talks about the foolish resistance to all things supernatural in contemporary Western cultures (*Breaking Dawn*, 715–16). This hyperrationalism is helpful in one way, he notes, as it keeps the vampires from being discovered since so many people do not believe that vampires exist. On the other hand, worries Aro, this is a culture in which the unchecked growth of science bound to technology has led to the development of weapons of mass destruction that threaten to destroy the planet, including even the immortals (*Breaking Dawn*, 715–16). So we have Aro, an utterly vile, sadistic vampire, demonstrating a more sensitive understanding of ecological interdependence than does Charlie, Bella's own father.

Salvation as the Journey to Faith

Even though Carlisle, Edward, and Bella have no interest in organized religion, they clearly have spiritual commitments. The spiritual journey is a theme subtly woven through all the plots and subtexts of salvation in Twilight. First there is Carlisle's path, in which he uses his supernatural strength to bring healing and peace to the world. Carlisle's spirituality emerges from his rejection of his clergy father's harsh religion. But Carlisle trusts in the existence of a good and merciful God, and he hopes for eternal salvation even for vampires who choose to live a moral life.

Edward has a faith journey, too, in which he gives his heart to Bella and overcomes his fear of damnation. Edward's fear is not for himself but for Bella. He wants his beloved to have a good life not only in mortality but also in eternity. As the story unfolds, Edward comes to believe that the best, most saving work in Bella's life is for her to become a vampire like himself, especially during the crisis of Renesmee's birth.

For Edward virtue is a matter of life choices in which he uses his saving power now, in this world, to protect his family and friends and to avoid doing evil to humankind. Both Carlisle and Edward fully reflect the LDS concept of "agency" or moral freedom, which every human being has and according to which every human being will be judged. Edward shows no progress to speak of in his understanding of God, but he advances in living his own vision of virtue.

By contrast, Charlie's faith journey is pitiful, mirroring other elements of his ineffectual life. Near the end of the fourth novel Charlie witnesses Jacob phase into a werewolf. Jacob tells the stunned sheriff that the world is quite different than Charlie thought, but that Charlie can ignore the truth and act as if nothing has changed (*Breaking Dawn*, 496). Jacob's advice to Charlie is reminiscent of a theme in the movie *The Matrix*, in which Neo (and others) have a choice to swallow the truth or willfully believe a lie. Neo chooses the truth. The traitor in the story, Cypher, chooses the pleasures of illusion.[12] Like Cypher, our Charlie chooses to know as little as possible. He prefers ignorance. We do not see in Charlie—a Lutheran—any expression of belief in a Great Sin, or in holiness, or in God, or even in choosing to embrace truth when he sees it. He stumbles along, basically unchanged by the end of the last book. Perhaps his purpose in this story is to help readers see how foolish it is to choose comfort over faith, safety over adventure.

This brings us to Bella. More than any other character, we see Bella move through her many religious doubts and irritations into emerging faith. Hers is a spirituality that is more like Edward's than Carlisle's, more connected to how life is lived in this world than to what happens in the next. Bella makes this transition by being a sojourner in community with the Cullens and the Quileutes, who are in this story the "people of faith." Her journey forward begins with Carlisle's testimony as he stitches her injured arm at the opening of *New Moon*. Even though Bella doesn't accept Carlisle's beliefs about God right away, her heart is softened toward him and all the Cullens in regard to their spirituality as she realizes how important God is to their decision to avoid human blood.

After she is married and pregnant, Bella realizes that something bigger than her relationship with Edward is unfolding. The dreams, the visions, the amazing fact of the supernatural all around her begin to convince her that she inhabits a larger story, a metanarrative, and it really is going somewhere. She names her awakening spiritual consciousness "faith" (*Breaking Dawn*, 190).

At the end of *Breaking Dawn,* as Bella, Edward, and the other vampires and werewolves await the final showdown with the Volturi, Bella still wonders if there will be an afterlife (*Breaking Dawn*, 652). She is convinced that they are not strong enough to win the battle against such formidable odds. She knows that in all likelihood they will suffer the fate of other vampires who have perished at the hands of the Volturi. They will be tortured, dismembered, and then burned to ashes. She cannot imagine what might come after this second death, so even at the potential end of her immortal life, Bella exhibits deep uncertainty about God, salvation, and heaven. Nonetheless, in her own way she has progressed into a deeper life of virtue as she understands it, becoming an agent of salvation and reconciliation among those she loves in this world.

Why it Matters

Twilight movie posters don't focus on theology, emphasizing instead Edward's brooding gaze and Jacob's chiseled pecs. Readers love Twilight first and foremost because this story is an action-packed romance. But we make a great mistake if we think that the theology of the series doesn't matter. Twilight is steeped in the spiritual quest and uncertainties of an entire generation. The Great Sins of Carlisle, Edward, and Bella reflect the offense that so many young adults feel toward the church, and for good reason. The hunger that Edward and Bella experience for a love that will last forever is more than a romantic yearning. It is the core of the human condition to have "eternity set in our hearts" (Eccl. 3:11, NIV.).

In the next chapter we will build on what we have discovered about temptation, sin, forbidden fruit, salvation, and heaven in Twilight to consider the presence of authoritarian institutions and leaders in this saga. These, too, reflect the commitments and growing resistance of young adults to all institutions that oppress others in the name of the common good.

Chapter Seven

Those Who Must Be Obeyed
The Volturi and the Corruption of Power

The first time we read of the Cullens a mere handful of pages into *Twilight,* we encounter the language of the angelic. The Cullens are beautiful in the manner of angels in a Renaissance masterpiece. With their marble skin, stunning hair, and mesmerizing eyes they are "devastatingly, inhumanly beautiful" (*Twilight*, 19). When they are in the room, it is hard to look away, partly because of their appearance and partly because of their unspoken power. Several times Meyer uses the word "angel" to describe how Bella sees Edward.

That word—*angel*—is the core of the word we translate as "evangelism" in English. The prefix *eu* means "good," as in "euphoric." An angel is a messenger. To be an ev-angel-ist is to be a messenger with good news. Indeed as the story unfolds, the Cullens do become evangelists of much that is good. Through word and deed they bring glad tidings to Bella about the importance of family, self-denial, a life dedicated to the greater good of the world, and faith that even vampires might go to heaven. As we've seen, the Cullens are the story's archetypal Good Family; Carlisle is the character with the most clearly defined faith in God; and Edward overcomes his thirst for Bella's blood with an even greater commitment to her safety. The world *is* made better by their family's love. The angels in this story are vampires. To underscore this connection, Beth Felker Jones's book about Twilight—*Touched by a Vampire*—plays on the title of a popular television series, *Touched by an Angel.*

But not every vampire in the Twilight saga is loving, and not all the news is good. Most of the undead are bloodthirsty killers. In the manner of Satan in the Bible (2 Cor. 11:14), the worst vampires of all, the Volturi, pose as angels of light. In outlining their position and power in the story, Meyer offers a harsh critique of religious and political oppression, especially when it masquerades as concern for the greater good.

Where It All Began

The first time Bella sees a picture of the Volturi, she is at the Cullens' home admiring their many works of art. Edward points to the largest painting, which appears to be a scene from antiquity, perhaps a story from the Bible or Greek mythology, even though it was actually painted only a few hundred years ago. Several people in vivid robes stand among a series of marble pillars (*Twilight*, 339). As Bella leans in for a closer look, she notices to her amazement that one of the figures is Carlisle.

Edward explains to her that when Carlisle first became a vampire in the seventeenth century, he spent several decades with the Volturi. Unlike the "sewer wraiths" who live in London, the Volturi are cultured vampires. Carlisle met them while he was in Italy at the university. Although initially attracted to what appeared to be their civilized, refined ways (*Twilight*, 340), he soon saw the truth behind their aristocratic façade. Beneath their love of art, music, and all things beautiful, the Volturi were as ruthless as any despot. Ultimately, Edward says, Carlisle and the Volturi parted ways because they tried to "cure" Carlisle of his "unnatural" aversion to human blood while he tried to evangelize them to his peaceful way of life. Their differences could not be overcome. This is our first narrative clue that the Volturi are not what they seem.

The image that the Volturi project is one of nobility with religious overtones. According to Edward, they are the largest coven in the world and are something like a royal family (*New Moon*, 19). The second-largest coven is Carlisle's family, a factor that plays into the story line in important ways.

Headquartered in Volterra, Italy, the three male vampires who lead the Volturi are Aro, Marcus, and Caius. Like Carlisle, each of them has, according to Bella, "the face of a seraph" (*New Moon*, 20), a special kind of angelic being in the Bible (see Isa. 6:2). Seraphs are the highest of angels in medieval Christian theology, the ones who stand by the throne of God in Revelation 4:4–8 crying, "Holy, holy, holy" into eternity. The word *seraph* means "burning, fiery light," so throughout millennia theologians have pondered the biblical image of seraphim adjacent to the throne of God, chanting the *Sanctus*, blazing with white hot love. The use of "seraphim" to describe the Volturi is indeed ironic.

In addition to the unholy trinity of Aro, Marcus, and Caius there are two childlike vampires—Jane and Alec—who complete the "family" of five. The "witch twins" have terrifying powers to cause the worst pain imaginable and to take away all sensory capacity, and they look just alike. The Volturi have a vampire police force as well, made of up nine male guards, plus the wives of Aro and Caius, making their company formidable. Interestingly, as Alice provides this information to Bella while they prepare for their mission to prevent Edward from suicide, she describes the Volturi as a "family of five" without including the wives of Aro and Caius (*New Moon*, 428). As noted in chapter 2, these wives are stereotypical meek females with powerful husbands.

Aro, Caius, and Marcus are three thousand years old when Bella learns of their existence. Alice explains to Bella that usually vampires cannot tolerate living together, except for mated pairs. They are too competitive and ruthless for community. But because of the advanced age of the three, she says, they may have developed the capacity to coexist in a large coven (*New Moon*, 429). Alternatively, suggests Alice, the five may be able to get along with all the others because of the special powers that they can use to control others. It may be a coercive togetherness. But it could simply be their love of power, she concludes, that keeps them together. Alice never suggests that they are peaceful.

Clue number two: the Volturi love power. This contrasts sharply with the Cullens and their power of love. The Volturi rose to power over millennia, assuming a position of leadership for themselves.

Their role is to enforce the one cardinal rule of vampire life: to keep vampires' existence a secret from humans. As Alice explains to Bella, the Volturi have imposed martial law, punishing all transgressors of the rule (*New Moon*, 430). They show no mercy, annihilating any vampire or human who puts vampires at risk of exposure. They also take exquisite pleasure in their gruesome role, as we eventually learn in *Eclipse* and *Breaking Dawn*. By these measures the Volturi have managed to live without detection in the city of Volterra for three thousand years.

Part of the way they escape detection is by protecting Volterra from crime and by bringing human prey in from the outside. That is, groups of tourists come from around the world to visit the ancient buildings of Volterra and to learn of the folktale of St. Marcus driving the vampires from the city some 1,500 years earlier. (Yes, this is the same Marcus who is actually part of the Volturi, but the gullible humans do not know this; rather than vanquishing the vampires in the city, Marcus became one of them and then went underground.) Lured by a sexy vampire named Heidi into chambers deep below the city, the hapless travelers are then locked in a room where they become victims of a feeding frenzy for "St. Marcus" and the other Volturi (*New Moon*, 482–84). This is not a children's tale.

Aro, the chief spokesman and leader for the Volturi, is a collector of all forms of beauty, talent, and rare things, both living and inanimate (*Breaking Dawn*, 532). His most treasured collection is comprised of vampires with special gifts, whom he regards as objects to use. It is how Jane and Alec, the sadistic young pair, came to be part of the Volturi. Aro especially covets the powers of Edward, Alice, and Bella (who even as a human in *New Moon* exhibits a powerful talent for mental self-protection), wanting to use them in his small but deadly empire (*New Moon*, 476–77).

Saints in White Hats

Although they are described as a type of royal family, and throughout most of the novels Edward insists that they aren't supposed to be viewed as villains but as "the foundation of our peace and civilization," the fact is that in the vampire world, the Volturi are as bad as it gets (*Breaking Dawn*, 580). Like human dictators they police the undead world through intimidation, violence, torture, and terrorism. Biblical scholar Sandra Gravett explores parallels between the Volturi and the wicked Roman Empire in the book of Revelation.[1]

As the Cullens and their friends prepare to resist the Volturi at the end of *Breaking Dawn,* two Romanian vampires, Stefan and Vladimir, tell Bella the story of their own subjugation at the hands of the Volturi. At one time the Romanians were very powerful. They sat in their castles and had to extend virtually no effort because everyone, including (unsuspecting) prey and diplomats, came to seek their favor (*Breaking Dawn*, 631). As Vladimir explains, because of their power they came to think of themselves as gods. But as the centuries rolled on and they increasingly saw themselves as deities, they slowly began to "petrify." Their bodies grew still, and their eyes developed the same dusty film that Bella has noticed in Aro's eyes.

As the Volturi rose to power. they attacked Stefan and Vladimir, burning their castles and driving the Romanians from their elite positions. No longer self-defined gods and humbled by their displacement at the hands of the Volturi, the Romanians became free from power-induced blindness, and their eyes lost their dusty film.

Once in control the Volturi began to search for and destroy other vampires who failed to serve Volturi interests, but always in the name of the common good, claiming that they were protecting vampires from human detection. This was done with quasi-religious authority, with the Volturi "putting on white hats" and calling themselves "saints," as Stefan reveals (*Breaking Dawn*, 658).

Armies of Newborns

Sometimes Volturi oppression takes the form of warfare, as in the events leading up to Jasper's conversion. As Jasper begins to tell his story to Bella, he shows her his battle-scarred arm. The only thing that can scar a vampire is another vampire's venom. Jasper's body is covered with a thousand bites. While Bella recoils with the violence that Jasper endured, he explains the history of the Southern Wars (*Eclipse*, 287–300).

Unlike the "civilized" north, in the south (meaning the southern United States and down into Central and South America), vampires have turf wars to control the "feeding" zones where humans are plentiful. Over the centuries the southern vampires battled it out, trying various methods to eliminate competitors and control densely populated cities. Eventually a vampire named Benito who came from north Texas massacred covens close to Houston, then moved into Mexico, where he took out even stronger vampires in Monterrey (*Eclipse*, 289). (When you think of Benito, think "drug lord" and "cartel," an unforgiveable racial stereotype: the one Hispanic person in Meyer's four-volume series is a criminal.)

The secret of Benito's success was that he created an army of newborn vampires, something no one had ever done. The newborns are crazed with thirst, impossibly strong, and uncontrollable. They kill other vampires and devour humans. As Benito and his army continued to move south, dominating more and more of Mexico, vampires in the south responded in kind to protect themselves, creating their own armies. Jasper explains to Bella that the carnage was beyond description, decimating both human and vampire populations of Mexico (*Eclipse*, 290). Humans explained this reign of death as a plague of disease, of course.

As the slaughter increased exponentially, the Volturi finally moved in. Beginning with Benito, the Volturi and their guard took down all the newborns and every vampire who had created them. The genocide took a full year. Though the Volturi retreated after nearly every vampire in Mexico was destroyed, before long other vampires came to Mexico, and the previous turf-lord culture resumed. This time the vampires were much more careful, controlling how many newborns they created and being more selective about which humans they changed. As long as the human population remained ignorant of the vampires' existence, and the little gangs of Mexican vampires remained too small to be a threat, the Volturi left the southern vampires alone.

As Jasper recounts these horrors, Bella suddenly realizes that he had been created to serve in a vampire army. His face is tormented in a way that she has never seen for the Cullen family member whose gift is to bring feelings of peace. Like any veteran with posttraumatic stress, Jasper tries to shake off the painful memories. He tells Bella, "We owe the Volturi for our present way of life" (*Eclipse*, 291). Without the Volturi stepping in, the carnage would have become global. Though Jasper lost his human life as an act of violence in war, he is grateful for the police work of the Volturi. Jasper, like Edward, prefers a positive spin on the dark lords.

As time goes by, however, Jasper and Edward change their minds. Their disillusionment is driven by revelations having to do with the problem of immortal children.

Those Who Are Forbidden

Far back into the mists of antiquity certain vampires, for inexplicable reasons, began to create immortals from toddlers. Like all vampires the little ones were predatorily attractive, so that everyone who looked upon them instantly loved them. Yet the wee tykes could not be tamed or taught to observe the one cardinal rule. They were frozen developmentally at whatever age they had been when they were bitten. The result of this was that the children were utterly deadly. As any parent knows, the "terrible twos" is the stage of development when children begin to assert their will. Tantrums are frequent. The cherubic-looking vampire tots left a swath of destruction that put vampires everywhere at risk (*Breaking Dawn*, 33–34). People were beginning to talk.

The Volturi watched carefully to see how the immortal children behaved and whether there was any way to civilize them. Ultimately Caius decided the little ones had to be destroyed because they were hopelessly wild. A great slaughter ensued around the world, with vampire covens fighting to the end to protect their children. Aro kept two of them for further observation, ever the collector of rare things. But in the end even those two had to be destroyed. Immortal children became taboo.

One of the ancient vampires—the mother of the Denali coven of Tanya, Kate, and Irina—created an immortal child whom she kept a secret from her other children. (The Denali family are close friends of the Cullens, and like the Cullens they are also vegetarians.) When the Volturi learned of the boy, they wasted no time and went to Denali to exact punishment. When interrogated, Tanya, Kate, and Irina clearly knew nothing about the child or that the Volturi had already taken him and their mother prisoner. The Volturi's punishment was swift and merciless: the mother held the little one in her arms while they both burned to death. Tanya, Kate, and Irina had to look on. Caius wanted to burn the three sisters as well, even though they had been proven innocent (*Breaking Dawn*, 33–36), but Aro let them live. The Denali sisters never got over their horror at what their mother had done, nor had they forgiven her. Because of her choice to create "the unmentionable bane," she orphaned her three daughters. As a result they became zealots regarding the law against immortal children (*Breaking Dawn*, 547).

Fast-forward to the future, with Bella now transformed into a Cullen, a vampire, *and a mother*. Irina comes to the Cullens to seek reconciliation after the death of her mate, Laurent, but as she approaches, she sees Renesmee playing with Bella while out on a hunt. She is enraged to see Jacob, the wolf who murdered Laurent, friendly with a Cullen. When she realizes what Renesmee must be, she snaps. A forbidden child, she thinks, the appalling evil that led to her mother's death (*Breaking Dawn*, 536–39). Overwhelmed with grief and jumping to conclusions, Irina goes to the Volturi, unleashing the final, cataclysmic events of the story.

Resistance

Just as Bella had seen in countless nightmares and visions, the entire company of the Volturi with all their guards and even their wives (who have never before left the towers of Volterra), advance upon Forks to destroy the Cullens—all but one special member of the Good Family: Alice. The Volturi have been waiting for this opportunity, because Carlisle's influence and the size of his coven are a threat to their hegemonic power. Though Aro would love to have Edward among the Volturi, Alice is the Cullen whom Aro covets more than he has ever wanted anything. Seeing into the future, Alice alerts her family of impending doom. They all assume that what Aro wants is punishment for the existence of what he mistakenly believes is an immortal child, not realizing that Renesmee is actually a rapidly growing half-vampire, half-human child.

Immobilized by dread, the Cullens at first cannot decide what to do. They lack the numbers and strength to overwhelm the Volturi in a fight. Then Emmett suggests a novel idea: why not bring other vampires from around the world? There are plenty who seem to have issues with the Volturi. Even if the others don't fight, they could serve as witnesses that Renesmee is not an immortal child. With strength of numbers perhaps the witnesses can make the Volturi stop long enough to listen to the truth—that Renesmee is growing and that she is warm and without venom.

Soon the plan is underway. The Cullens fan out for an international search to assemble all the vampires they can find who will come and bear witness. As Edward and Bella prepare for the coming showdown, Edward explains that Eleazar is a vampire who used to serve in the Volturi guard. He will be an especially helpful ally for the Cullens because of his past. When Bella questions how Eleazar ever got away from the Volturi alive, Edward chides her, saying that members of the Volturi guard are prestigious and serve in the guard by choice (*Breaking Dawn*, 580). He adds that only criminals think the Volturi are evil. He is soon to be disabused of that thought.

As the friends begin to assemble from around the world, Eleazar included, they strategize the best way to convince the Volturi that Renesmee is not a forbidden child. Despite Edward's previous statements about the Volturi being the foundation of peace and safety in the vampire world, and Jasper's gratitude for the Volturi ending the Southern Wars, it quickly becomes clear that many vampires do not entirely trust the Volturi or their motives. There has been too much violence in the past. They decide they must plan for battle even while hoping for the unlikely outcome of a peaceful resolution. As Tanya says to Kate, the plan to fight is little more than a "suicide mission" (*Breaking Dawn*, 593).

While preparing for battle, Eleazar and Edward try to unravel the mystery of why so many of the Volturi are on their way to Forks. Eleazar's special power is to recognize the gifts in other vampires. (He has, in spiritual terms, the gift of discernment.) When he was part of the Volturi guard, his responsibility was to search for vampires with unique gifts that could help Aro and the Volturi.

Every hundred years or so Eleazar would discover a rare vampire with potential for Aro's guard. Inevitably the small coven in which the gifted vampire lived would come under judgment for some allegedly unpardonable crime, and the Volturi and Aro would go to carry out the execution. One by one the members of the coven would die, and then at the last minute Aro would extend mercy to the one with the gift. That vampire would then be absorbed into the guard, grateful to be alive (*Breaking Dawn*, 601–2).[2] As Eleazar shares this information, he and Edward realize that the whole contingent of Volturi are coming to Forks for one reason: to get Alice, the vampire whose gifts Aro covets. Renesmee's offensive existence is simply a ruse. Renesmee's destruction and the deaths of other Cullens will be marginal to the Volturi's actual goal: capturing Alice and her power to see the future (*Breaking Dawn*, 604). If they can get Alice and destroy the Cullens in the process, their power will be virtually unassailable. The threat of the Cullens' countercultural way of life will be suppressed.

Moreover, they discover, the guard named Chelsca is responsible for the seeming unity among the Volturi. Her special gift is to sever and forge emotional ties among people. It is Chelsea's power, not prestige or free will as Edward had assumed, that keeps the guard loyal and enables the Volturi to coexist in such large numbers.

In the face of such impregnable opposition the Cullens would need every ally they could find. Soon a formidable alliance of twenty-seven vampires gathers at the Cullens' home. Included among these are Stefan and Vladimir, the Romanians whose appearance and voices are chillingly similar to those of Aro, Marcus, and Caius. They are the first to openly name their desire to bring down the Volturi (*Breaking Dawn*, 626).

The Romanians vehemently state their hope that the Volturi will fall and that the rest of the vampire world will wake up to the charade of the Volturi's peaceful intent. Though the Romanians have a personal vendetta, their words force the doubting vampires to think about the evidence of the Volturi's abuse of power. Finally, one by one the fearsome guests begin to declare their willingness to fight. Their language is that of an insurrection. "It appears I have to win the right to be free," says Benjamin, a likeable young fellow. Garrett agrees: "Here's to freedom from oppression!" (*Breaking Dawn*, 659).

Then the Volturi arrive, bringing their own pack of witnesses, a vampire lynch mob, lusting for vigilante justice. As Bella explains, the Volturi have gathered more than forty gullible vampires and convinced them that an immortal child had been created and that in bringing the guilty vampires to justice there might be a fight. "It was clear that this motley, disorganized horde . . . was the Volturi's own kind of witness," she realizes. She understands that the "witnesses" would then be tasked with spreading the word that the criminals had been justly executed and that the Volturi had been nothing but fair. She also senses that the visitors have another goal in mind: "They hoped for more than just an opportunity to witness—they wanted to help tear and burn" (*Breaking Dawn*, 681). No one, not even the optimistic Carlisle, can doubt any more that the Volturi have sinister plans—securing their power, acquiring more gifted vampires for their guard, and eliminating anyone who gets in their way.

But their plan backfires when the witnesses for the Volturi see Caius murder Irina, the one who reported the existence of Renesmee. Her death is a calculated act of terrorism intended to cow the witnesses and ignite a battle with the Cullens. It has the opposite effect. The lynch mob realizes it has been duped by the Volturi.

As Aro and Caius continue to posture, Garrett requests permission to speak. When he was human, he had been an American Revolutionary patriot. Addressing the Volturi witnesses, he names the truth that everyone now can see. The Volturi have come to destroy the Cullens because the Volturi regard them as a threat. With courage reminiscent of Braveheart, Garrett shouts the virtues of the Cullens who are a *"family* and not [a] *coven"* (*Breaking Dawn*, 717). He has studied their peaceful way of life, founded on the principle of personal sacrifice for the well-being of others, and the marvelous absence of aggression in their posture toward one another and the rest of the world (*Breaking Dawn*, 717–18). There is no way the Cullens are planning to overthrow anyone, but the Volturi want to kill them anyway. They fully intend to wipe out the Good Family.

Gaining momentum, Garrett raises questions to the witnesses with stunning power. Are the Volturi really protectors of the vampire world, or are they power-hungry despots? Everyone now knows the answer to that question. "The Volturi care nothing for the death of the child," he spits. "They seek the death of our free will" (*Breaking Dawn*, 719).

In the end the Cullens win out because they have Bella's shield of protection and because enough truth has been told that the Volturi have to leave to save face. Amazingly, other than Irina no one dies. As the ragtag group of would-be resistance fighters celebrates their victory, they agree that the Volturi will be back. The dark lords will try to pick off the resistors separately or resort to some other scheme. But their control has unquestionably been broken. The power of the Cullens' love saves the day.

Sandra Gravett likens the Cullens' peaceful victory to that of the early Christians who resisted the Roman Empire not with military might but by creating an alternative society that modeled a new relationship between the vulnerable and those in power.[3] Through challenging the existing social order with nonviolent resistance, the Cullens usher in a better day for the world.

The Volturi as Archetypes of Colonial Oppression

In Meyer's world the Volturi represent colonial oppression, specifically the type of colonization that is both political and religious. They colonize geographically and demographically through controlling the size and location of covens worldwide and through "harvesting" for themselves the best and brightest vampires with special gifts. To achieve all of this control they more subtly colonize the minds of vampires everywhere through intimidation, violence, and deception. By putting on white hats and calling themselves "saints," a description offered by Stefan (*Breaking Dawn*, 658), they create an ethical illusion, posing as the arm of justice that protects peaceful vampire life. But their ethic is entirely self-serving. Other vampires are objects to be used or thrown away. Dissidents are brutally repressed. When things begin to get too chaotic, genocide is the preferred option.

The Volturi in many ways function like modern despots, but they are even more like political and religious institutions that fall prey to the "powers and principalities," corrupted by their own power so that instead of serving the people who created them, the people become prey for the gaping maw of the institution.

In the Volturi we also see an anti-Catholic sensibility to Meyer's inherent critique of organized religion. Think of the church that was born of a Nazarene carpenter among a disempowered people on the margins of empire. Look forward a few centuries to see that church become an empire of its own, complete with a powerful male hierarchy dressed in robes, headquartered *in Italy*, and with a penchant for extraordinary cruelty against those who are different. The Inquisition; the brutal repression of mystics, saints, and prophets who dared to ask hard questions of the church; the public torture and execution of peace-loving dissidents such as the Anabaptists; the appalling church-sanctioned genocides of indigenous people during colonial expansion; the church's participation in slavery and its widespread, systemic oppression of women—all of these forms of institutional religious oppression are ideas that eddy around the dusty robes of the Volturi.

And then there is the problem of St. Marcus, who in Meyer's imagination is Father Marcus, the Christian missionary who went to Volterra to drive out all the vampires but was bitten and became part of the unholy trio. He is like televangelists who obsess over sexual sin in their preaching and are then exposed for their own sexual failings. To hunt vampires is to risk becoming one.

But there is more for us to learn from St. Marcus. Every single time Marcus is mentioned in this story he is, quite honestly, bored. He is without expression, blank, uncaring, detached. Psychologists call this "flat affect," a sign that something is not right in a person's head. Marcus goes along with Aro and Caius in their devious killing plots because there is nothing better to do. He is in fact a sociopath, one who has lost his conscience. Marcus is the ultimate picture of clergy gone bad, demonic in his complicity with worldly powers. He drinks the life out of others, but he feels no pleasure, no remorse, no shame, nothing. He is dead.

What is the invitation of these disturbing themes? How did the Volturi become so evil? It's all about the corrupting influence of power. Perhaps the Volturi started with the best of intents. The novels are not entirely clear about this. But as we see in Stefan and Vladimir's story, what leads to the Volturi's corruption is their increasingly bloated sense of their own deity. They feel entitled to do whatever they wish to do.

Who are the real "saints in white hats?" The Cullens, of course—the Good Family, especially Carlisle. The way the Cullens break Volturi power is the way readers (and the church) can engage the colonizing oppressors in our world. It is through speaking the truth to power, as Carlisle does, and creating strong communities of truth and reconciliation wherever we can. The Cullens have incredible power precisely because they eschew controlling others.

The Cullens' victory over the Volturi never could have happened without the Quileutes, the Irish coven, the Amazons, the Romanians, and the many others who assemble for the final battle at the conclusion of *Breaking Dawn*. It could not have happened without Bella's protective shield or Alice's perceptive vision. But Carlisle is the linchpin in this motley crew. He won the day through a long history of loving his neighbors. For centuries Carlisle has cultivated friendships with all manner of living things, respecting and listening to everyone's views wherever he goes. Carlisle succeeds through choosing peace over violence, and negotiation over control. He develops an alternative family to open the imaginations of vampires everywhere. Violence and mayhem are not the only way, not even for monsters.

Carlisle is the archangel in this story. He is an evangelist for the Good Life whose life, teaching, and sacrifices are woven of one fabric of love. He not only bears glad tidings of peace but also invites others to join him on the journey and take up the way of reconciliation. In the next and final chapter we will reflect on that healing path, which is the theological capstone of this story.

Chapter Eight

Engaging the Powers
The Reconciliation of All Things

When I was in junior high, my brother and I spent many Saturday afternoons mesmerized by old vampire movies. White-knuckled, we watched as the handsome vampire hunter descended the staircase into the crypt, wooden stake and crucifix in hand. The sun was about to go down, so there was scarcely a moment to lose! At twilight the undead would arise. Would the man with the stake end the reign of terror or become part of it? (And it was always a man. This was before Buffy.)

Vampire stories are nothing new. Throughout the world for millennia, tales of vampires and werewolves have functioned as powerful myths to personify monstrous evil. Unlike many other legendary monsters, vampires and werewolves serve as archetypes for ordinary people consumed by the demonic. Their living hell begins with an external bite but quickly progresses to full possession and control from within. Those who are bitten cannot go back; they cannot heal themselves. They are hopelessly doomed to create more monsters by passing their affliction on to others. Vampires and werewolves are given over to evil whether they chose it for themselves or not. Usually they have not. Ordinarily their only hope is to find freedom from their bondage in death.

Traditional werewolf and vampire stories offer readers a vicarious experience of spiritual warfare—engaging the "powers, principalities, and forces of wickedness" that infest the world (Eph. 6:12 KJV).[1] These stories nearly always include a savior figure who fights the monster at great personal peril but who usually triumphs, freeing the village (and often a pretty woman) from oppression. So these stories have savior figures, sacrifice, risk, and the hope of liberation. Just as the hero goes among the undead to protect the well-being of vulnerable people, readers are challenged to take risks and go to dark places in order to bring healing to the world. Yet the task of "going to the crypt" is fraught with danger. Vampires and werewolves bear a contagion. Their hunters can be bitten and suffer a fate worse than death. The lesson is clear: the one who judges the possessed is the one most likely to become the next monster.

This is one of the reasons the Harry Potter novels are so compelling and are popular with many of the same people who love Twilight. Harry must constantly struggle against the wicked Lord Voldemort, who has willingly given himself over to the dark side. As the story unfolds, young Harry realizes the shocking truth that he and Lord Voldemort are connected in a deep, primeval way, for their wands contain feathers from the same magical phoenix. By the sixth novel Harry's blood has mingled with Voldemort's. The evil that resides in Voldemort calls to Harry, so that at times Harry actually sees through the eyes of Voldemort and feels the dark lord's hatred as if it were his own. Will Harry overcome Voldemort's evil with good? Or will he succumb to the same demonic lust for power?

Readers of all ages find such stories irresistible because they raise a timeless question, one that is inherent in the good-versus-evil drama of Twilight: How does one resist evil when it takes human form? Can reconciliation happen in the face of overwhelming evil?

The Powers

Resisting evil is what Pentecostals call spiritual warfare. "For our struggle is not against flesh and blood, but against the rulers, against the authorities, against the powers of this dark world and against the spiritual forces of evil in the heavenly realms," writes the author of Ephesians (6:12, NIV). The way to resist the "powers and principalities" (in the language of the KJV) is to put on the "whole armor of God" and to "stand fast." Why does Ephesians specify that our enemy is "the powers" and not flesh and blood? Because it is very tempting to think otherwise. In our resistance of evil it is all too easy to demonize other people, to make judgments about others that dehumanize, objectify, and scapegoat them. Therein lies the root of every crime against humanity that has been done in the name of God, from inquisitions to witch hunts to pogroms.

For this reason the apostle Paul writes that Christians have been called to be ambassadors of reconciliation (2 Cor. 5:16–21). We are no longer to view other people as we once did—with the old stereotypes, labels, judgments, and exclusions. Now we are to live as if the redemption of Christ for all people is real. One of the major themes of both Ephesians and Colossians is the reconciliation of all things in Christ: "For in him all the fullness of God was pleased to dwell, and through him God was pleased to reconcile to himself all things, whether on earth or in heaven, by making peace through the blood of his cross" (Col. 1:19–20). Thus reconciliation extends beyond human beings to creation itself.

What is extraordinary about the Twilight series is that the monsters—vampires and werewolves—become reconciled with one another in the process of working together to *protect* human life. The usual mythic formula is turned on its head. Twilight is not the usual tale of vampires and werewolves as demonized humans, the familiar story I watched with my brother when we were kids. It is also different from the story of the Gerasene man in Mark 5, whose exorcism results in the death of a herd of pigs. On the contrary, as already noted the Cullens and Quileutes are angelic, protective, and good, despite and in some ways *because of* their lot in life. The humans (especially those who are divorced) are the ones with issues. Within this ironic twist we find Stephenie Meyer's best social and religious critique.

Carlisle's father epitomizes the evil that takes place when Christians decide that their enemy *is* flesh and blood and that violence is the best "final solution." It was Carlisle's father's violent crusade that resulted in his own son becoming a vampire. For this reason Carlisle devotes his life to being a healer, cultivating peace and reconciliation wherever he goes. Carlisle is the character who first initiates the original treaty between the Quileutes and the Cullens (*Twilight*, 125–26; *Eclipse*, 118–19).

Yet as important as Carlisle is to the process, the biggest hero of reconciliation in this story is our Bella. Intentionally and unintentionally, Bella brings together an array of people and creatures that have been at odds for centuries, uniting in her own family—even in her own body—those who were once enemies. For Bella, reconciliation is the natural work of love and has nothing to do with religion. Out of love, then, rather than religious sensibilities, Bella incarnates the deepest Christian theological commitment of the series. Bella is like Jesus, who

> has broken down the dividing wall, that is, the hostility between us. He has abolished the law with its commandments and ordinances, that he might create in himself one new humanity in place of the two, thus making peace, and might reconcile both groups to God in one body through the cross, thus putting to death the hostility through it. (Eph. 2:14–16)

That Bella accomplishes without religion what Christianity claims to be its central concern—the redemption and reconciliation of all that is broken by sin—is in itself a powerful critique of "organized religion." She represents many young adults I know and love who have given up on church altogether, finding it somewhere between irrelevant and inherently opposed to the kind of peaceful, reconciling social consciousness that is needed to heal our violent world.

A World in Need of Reconciliation

To appreciate the importance of Bella's reconciling work in Twilight we readers must review our own globalized, sociopolitical context. We have to own terrible words like *lynching, terrorism, racial profiling*, and *genocide*. Even though we are appalled by these evils, and even if we have never participated knowingly in any of them, we are still part of the human family in which these demonic events take place. We are family. All of us are hurt by these forms of violence, and we all bear some responsibility for these crimes against ourselves and against the earth and its nonhuman creatures. It is our shared task to heal these monstrous wounds.

Thanks to advanced weaponry and technological "progress," the twentieth century was arguably the most violent era in human history, and the twenty-first shows every sign of getting worse. During the past hundred years the world has met the likes of Joseph Stalin, Benito Mussolini, Adolf Hitler, Pol Pot, Idi Amin, and Augusto Pinochet, just to name a few. Under their dictatorships millions of men, women, and children experienced unspeakable atrocities, including imprisonment, torture, and murder.

And the violence is not limited to despotic rulers. Our world is riddled with abuse of all kinds: police brutality, human trafficking, human rights violations against undocumented workers, lynchings, violence against gay men and women, domestic violence, sexual abuse of children, factory farming of animals, the poaching and mutilation of gorillas and rhinos, and the list goes on.

Even when physical violence is absent, astonishing acts of hostility take place all around us every day through bullying—in the workplace, on the Internet, in church board meetings, in locker rooms, and on school playgrounds. How could anyone ever doubt the existence of evil? And how does one resist evil while hoping for and working toward the reconciliation of all things? The question is woven throughout Twilight.

Enemies

Like the Bible, Twilight does not address the origin of evil. It does not tell us how the first vampire came to be. Vampires are simply a given, as are werewolves. Aro, Caius, and Marcus are the oldest vampires in the story, dating back before the time of Christ, but with the exception of Marcus we do not know the details of their histories. Vladimir and Stefan are ancient too, having been subdued by the three Volturi leaders 1,500 years earlier (*Breaking Dawn*, 626).

The werewolves in this story are actually shape-shifters, we eventually discover. Their origins go back to the ancestors of Jacob Black and his people. Rather late in the story we learn that the real werewolves ("children of the moon") have been driven nearly to extinction by the Volturi. Aro explains the differences to Caius, who calls werewolves "our bitter enemies from the dawn of time" (*Breaking Dawn,* 626), and refers to the Quileute shape-shifters as an "infestation." Even so, the Quileute shape-shifters are consistently called werewolves by themselves and everyone else throughout the novels to the very end. What matters about the origins of shape-shifters in Twilight is that this species, unlike real werewolves, evolved specifically to destroy vampires. They are genetically programmed to kill the undead.

When the Cold Woman decimated a Quileute village generations before Jacob was born, the Quileute chief Taha Aki phased into the first Quileute "werewolf," and in that form, with the help of his self-sacrificing (some would say kamikaze) third wife and his two sons, destroyed the Cold Woman. From then on, any time vampires came even near Quileute land, the young men would involuntarily begin to phase into werewolves. Working as a pack with an alpha, they were more than capable of bringing down the craftiest of vampires.

Because the Quileutes' ability to phase into werewolves is a genetic adaptation to the threat of vampires, from the very beginning the two species have been mortal enemies. As Twilight unfolds and Bella reconnects with her childhood friend, Jacob Black, she learns about the legend of the Cold Ones. (Interestingly, Rebecca Housel notes that the name "Cullen" sounds like "Cold Ones."[2]) Jacob tells Bella about the treaty between the unusual group of Cold Ones and the Quileutes (*Twilight,* 125–26). We learn later, of course, that the Cullens are the oddballs of the vampire world, and that Carlisle is the agent of inter-species reconciliation. As long as the Cullens do not cross into Quileute lands, the Quileutes will leave them alone. Despite the treaty, however, there is deep mistrust on both sides and more than a little revulsion toward the "other." Quileutes find the sweet aroma of the vampires to be repulsive (*New Moon,* 377, is just one of many references to the vampire aroma in the series); similarly, vampires can barely stand the smell of the werewolves, whose stench is something like a wet, dirty dog (*New Moon*, 421).

Though Jacob recounts the legend in a manner that suggests he doesn't believe in Cold Ones or werewolves, he knows more than he reveals. In time Bella learns that the story is true, and when some of his male cousins and friends begin to behave strangely, Jacob undergoes a rude awakening.

Just as Meyer offers a strong message of reconciliation between hostile groups (werewolves and vampires), she also offers readers a chance to think about the problem of judging, labeling, and rejecting those who are different within our own groups. She does this by allowing readers to journey with Jacob through his coming of age as a werewolf. At first Jacob only half believes the old legend of the Cold Ones. Then Sam Uley begins to act weird, cutting his hair, sporting a new tattoo, and gathering to himself a small group of young men who begin to look and act like him. Jacob reacts with contempt, calling Sam a gang leader and sarcastically referring to Sam's friends as disciples and to the group as a cult. Jacob despises the way Sam and his buddies call themselves "protectors." Bella joins in on the labeling, viewing the group as a gang of racists when she realizes they harbor a deadly hatred of vampires (*New Moon*, 268). To her they are thugs.

Bella, the Ambassador of Reconciliation

Sam's hatred of vampires isn't Bella's first taste of antivampire racism, which occurs in *Twilight* (353) when Billy Black tells her to stop seeing Edward and to stay away from the rest of the Cullens. She later discovers with sorrow the ugly names the Cullen children and the Quileute werewolves use to demonize each other, epithets such as dog, bloodsucker, leech, and parasite (*Eclipse*, 33). (Carlisle and Esme never use these dehumanizing names, by the way. Such behavior is beneath them.) Until Jacob becomes a werewolf and finally lets Bella in on what has happened to him and tells her he was wrong about Sam Uley, Bella can only feel revulsion for werewolves. She cannot understand their hatred of the Cullens, whom she adores.

Not long after Bella realizes that Jacob has turned into a nasty vampire-hunting werewolf, she comes to visit him at his home in La Push, where she finds him asleep. Jacob's vulnerability and beauty, his goodness, all the things about him that made her cherish his friendship before he changed, overcome her feelings of disgust. She stops seeing him through labels and judgments and is able to love him once again, even though at this point in the story she wrongly thinks he has become a killer. She realizes that he is more than his werewolf "condition," an insight that is key to any kind of reconciliation between hostile parties (*New Moon*, 304). This is the beginning of her work of reconciliation between the Quileutes and the Cullens. It is not enough for them simply to agree not to kill each other. Bella is not satisfied until they are friends—until they are (gulp) *family*.

In *New Moon*, when Bella deepens her friendship with Alice, whom she loves, Jacob protests. Bella glosses over his resistance, letting him know she is capable of being friends with both of them (*New Moon*, 408–9). Bella tells Jacob that she simply doesn't care that he is a werewolf and that Edward is a vampire. She shouts that she is a Virgo and they can all be friends, eliciting laughter from Jacob (*Eclipse*, 130). Later she tells Edward (who throws a fit because she is friends with "unstable werewolves") that she is unwilling to ditch either of them based on their stereotypes of each other. "I am Switzerland," she insists, able to be peaceful toward those who are "other" (*Eclipse*, 143). Bella adds that if her human friend Angela turns out to be a witch, she, too, will be welcome in the mix.

In *Eclipse*, it is Bella's vulnerability that initially brings Jacob and Edward together in a tense agreement to make sure that Bella and Charlie are safe from Victoria. Though Edward and Jacob can barely restrain themselves from tearing each other apart, especially because they are both in love with Bella, their love for her enables them to work together to protect her.

Over time the uneasy cooperation between Edward and Jacob must extend to collaboration between all of the Cullens and all of the werewolves. When Victoria creates an army of newborns to kill Bella and the Cullens, the two clans agree to face their common enemy together (*Eclipse*, 380–81, 391–93). The werewolves have to humble themselves and learn from the Cullens how to defeat an army of newborns, a kind of enemy they have not yet encountered. The Cullens have to set aside their disgust at the smell of the werewolves in order to work together.

In a strange sequence of events during the battle with the newborns, Bella becomes hypothermic while hiding from Victoria in a meadow high on the mountain. Because Edward is by nature physically cold, he cannot hold her close for warmth. Jacob, whose body temperature is 108 degrees, comes to the rescue. As he climbs into Bella's sleeping bag, Edward can barely restrain his jealousy, especially because of Jacob's wisecracks (*Eclipse*, 490–91). (In the film version, Jacob boasts, "Let's face it . . . I'm hotter than you.") But they are able to save her from hypothermia together. Later in the fight when Victoria shows up at the hiding place with a male vampire named Riley, the young werewolf Seth works with Edward to kill both of them. This experience binds Edward and Seth together in genuine friendship, so much so that when Edward and Bella get married, Seth comes to the wedding and hugs Edward, whom he has come to truly love (*Breaking Dawn*, 53). Sue and Billy Black also come.

The painful work of reconciliation reaches a climax in *Breaking Dawn* with Bella's pregnancy and the birth of Renesmee. As noted in earlier chapters, by the time Bella marries Edward, Jacob is agonizingly in love with her, so he cannot stop protecting her and wanting her happiness even though he cannot have her. As Bella's disturbing pregnancy advances, the werewolves are outraged at what it is doing to Bella. They are, after all, irrevocably committed to protecting humans from vampires, and before their very eyes Bella, who is still a human at this point, is being consumed by her vampire fetus.

During this time Jacob has a breakthrough in his hatred for Edward. Seeing Bella suffer, Jacob suddenly realizes the depths of Edward's pain in watching Bella die every day, knowing that he, Edward, caused the pregnancy. For a moment Jacob forgets his own pain and feels empathy for his rival and enemy. He realizes that he needs to live beyond the confines of bigotry that has until this event kept him from being able to understand life from his hated enemy's point of view (*Breaking Dawn*, 176). Empathy for the "other" is an essential but often difficult element in forgiving others and being reconciled with those who have hurt us.

At the same time, Edward's agony at seeing Bella deteriorate and her unwillingness to sacrifice the pregnancy for her own survival cause him to urge Bella to marry Jacob and bear children with him so that she can live. Edward loves her so much he is willing to give her up in this way to save her life. Of course she does not accept this offer, but this impulse by Edward is part of the dynamic that leads to full reconciliation between the vampire Cullens and the werewolf Quileutes.

When the wolf pack, led by Sam Uley, begins to demonize the unborn child, calling her an "abomination" and other hateful words, Jacob cannot remain silent. Partly because of his love for Bella and partly because of his awakening empathy for Edward (*Breaking Dawn*, 199–212), Jacob opens his mind to a truth he has resisted until this time. Although Sam Uley was the first Quileute in Jacob's generation to phase into a werewolf, by birthright Jacob is supposed to be the alpha. Until this confrontation he has not allowed himself to exercise his role because he did not want the power or the leadership responsibility (*Breaking Dawn*, 209). He takes his rightful position as alpha of the pack and confronts Sam Uley. He vows to save Bella from the pack, then races to warn the Cullens and protect them from the rest of the pack being led by Sam. Seth goes with him. Eventually Leah comes, too (*Breaking Dawn*, 225).

After this, Esme welcomes Jacob's pack to the Cullen property, where she offers them food, clothing, and shelter (though the clothing stinks unbearably to the wolves) (*Breaking Dawn*, 272–73). Musing over the strange turn of events, with werewolves living at a vampire house to protect Bella from other werewolves, Jacob says, "This was the problem with hanging out with vampires—you got used to them. They started messing up the way you saw the world. They started feeling like friends" (*Breaking Dawn*, 284).

Eventually Edward tells Jacob he has come to think of him as a brother or, at the very least, a trusted comrade in arms (*Breaking Dawn*, 341). Bella's dream is being fulfilled. Former enemies are now family-like friends.

One last problem threatens the growing peace between Jacob and Edward as they begin to assemble vampires from around the world to prepare to resist the Volturi. Edward tells Jacob that the vampires from Denali and beyond may not agree to help if there are werewolves involved. The degree of suspicion and mistrust may be too deep to overcome. Jacob is deeply offended by this and has to work through complicated feelings to come to terms with the truth of Edward's words (*Breaking Dawn*, 567–68). In the end the species do work together with Renesmee's safety as their common goal. With the help of Bella's shield, they are able to avert war with the Volturi.

The final capstone of reconciliation that Bella brings about is through the birth of Renesmee. As a child of both races, Renesmee incarnates peace between vampires and humans. She is also the one on whom Jacob imprints, so her existence seals the formal and permanent peace between the Quileutes and the Cullens. The Quileutes are bound by tradition and duty to protect the ones with whom their young men imprint. Once Renesmee is of age and marries Jacob (a foregone conclusion, as we saw in chapter 2), she will be part of the Quileute community as well as half human/half vampire. All the hostile species will have been reconciled through Bella, fully enfleshed in Renesmee. As the story concludes, Bella, Edward, Renesmee, and Jacob are more than friends. They have become the next generation of the Good Family and have taken the meaning of "good family" to a much deeper level.

We Are Family

Early in this book I proposed that the Good Family was in fact a prototype of a small but potent faith community. In many ways the Cullens reflect the kind of compassion, self-discipline, and communal consciousness that should characterize any Christian family or congregation. What happens through the course of the four novels, with Bella as the catalyst, is that the Cullens' ethos is multiplied beyond their own family unit. The small-scale reconciliation that Bella instigates between Edward and Jacob results in the greater healing of enmity between species. Bella is able to lead the Cullen family beyond even the accomplishments of Carlisle so that where there was once mortal (or immortal) hatred there now exist mutual familial bonds of love and trust.

Sandra Gravett finds in the conclusion of *Breaking Dawn* an insightful parallel to the formation of the new heaven and new earth in Revelation 21:1–4, popularly known as the peaceable kingdom.[3] Though the Volturi are not judged for eternity, their power is subdued. Vampires, wolves, and humans now can share the same community, just like the predators and prey of Isaiah 11:6–9. This idea is foreshadowed in Edward's comment to Bella in *Twilight* (274): "And so the lion fell in love with the lamb."

As we move further into the twenty-first century, finding a way through religious, racial, gender, class, and other forms of bigotry must be a top priority for Christians. It is unacceptable for the church to tolerate, much less perpetuate, the Great Sins that Bella, Edward, and Carlisle rightly abhor. The epic task of salvation that faces the church today is to become a community whose members are ambassadors of reconciliation, hospitable people who truly love our neighbors.

For this to happen the church must take stock and repent of its many forms of prejudice and contempt within its own ranks. Christians must beat our ecclesiastical swords into plowshares, celebrating our theological diversity as gifts and working together in all the ways that we can to heal the wounds of the world. As Brian McLaren notes in *A New Kind of Christianity: Ten Questions That Are Transforming the Faith*, a new generation of Luthers are rising in the church, women and men who seek "honest, open, and charitable dialogue" to free the church from its captivity to forms of faith that dehumanize, demonize, and exclude those who are "other."[4] They are convinced that the church must respond to the greatest needs of the world because of the interconnectedness of all creation. They believe, in the manner of Francis of Assisi and many other saints and mystics, that all of creation, both living and nonliving things, belongs to God and must be cared for in God's name.

While the Twilight series is first and foremost a love story, it is much more than that. Tucked within its pages are the spiritual and social concerns, disappointments, and hopes of the next generation for a world in which a lion and lamb may nap together and a child and a viper can be friends. Twilight concludes with metaphorical glimpses of a world freed from the powers and principalities, from the terror of religious leaders who declare "holy" war. It is a redeemed world in which vampires, werewolves, and teenage girls belong to one another—a world made new through love, where we are all family.

Guide for Reflection and Discussion

This reflection guide could be used in several ways. An individual reader could use it to think more deeply about the Twilight series and raise questions about its treatment of theology, salvation, or power. It could also be a resource for many kinds of group conversation—for example, between mothers and daughters after reading the Twilight novels and watching the movies, or in a youth group setting. It could also be used very effectively for a Twilight weekend retreat for young people, with time during the retreat for viewing a portion or all of the movies in their entirety.

Finally, the guide could serve as a discussion starter for a small group of readers who want to discuss the novels from a specific standpoint of gender equality. These questions are intended to help readers, particularly girls and women, reflect on the many themes and subtexts relating to gender, sex, and power in the stories. Rather than looking for the "right" answers, this reflection guide is meant to open conversation about girls' and women's well-being, both in the novels and the world in which we live.

Introduction

1. The Twilight novels were written by Stephenie Meyer, a woman whom commentators often describe as a "Mormon housewife and mother," who had never published anything before. They seem surprised that a Mormon housewife and mother could produce a best-selling series of novels. What are the hidden assumptions in our culture about women of faith

134

who are wives and mothers that cause the commentators to be surprised?

2. Some Christians think that fiction about vampires, witches, wizards, or any other magical or supernatural creatures is inherently tainted and should not be read by Christians, or it will damage faith. What do you think about this belief?

3. What are some movies or books from popular culture other than the Twilight novels that have influenced your life in a spiritual or ethical way?

The Good Family

1. Messages about the importance of family in Twilight are in some ways exemplary from a Christian point of view. Stable, healthy families, after all, are the basic building blocks for strong communities. What constitutes a "good" family in the gospel according to Twilight? Who are they? What do they do that makes them "good"?

2. The Good Family in this story requires a mother, father, and children. What are the hidden implications in this arrangement? Is this a fair expectation for a family to be "good"?

3. Carlisle is the "head" of the Cullen family, which means it is a patriarchal family. What is your understanding of patriarchy? How is power distributed in patriarchal families? What are the embedded assumptions about women in patriarchal systems? In what ways did Jesus challenge patriarchy in his culture?

4. The only divorced people in this story—Charlie and Renee—are shown to be immature, dysfunctional, and inadequate as parents. How does this portrayal of divorced people compare with your experience of divorced adults?

I'm Only Half of Me

1. What are the hidden assumptions about being single in this series?

2. How did you feel the first time you read the part of the story

where Bella discovers that Sam mauled Emily, scarring her for life, but Emily forgave him and stayed with him anyway?

3. What would you do if you saw a friend being controlled or abused by her partner? What would you want your friend to do if she saw the control or abuse happening to you?
4. Where in your family and among your friends have you seen healthy boundaries and mutual respect between men and women?
5. How can families and the church more effectively prevent domestic violence and sexual abuse?

Is Twilight Bad News for Girls?

1. What are some of the stereotypes about women and girls found in this story?
2. What are some of the stereotypes about men and boys?
3. How did you feel about Bella when you began reading the books and found her tripping, falling, and running into things, all the while berating herself for her clumsiness and generally bad lot in life?
4. Bella functions like an adult when it comes to taking care of her parents in this story but needs to be taken care of by a man when it comes to herself. She frequently needs to be rescued, carried, fed, protected, or taught by a male. What are the messages in this portrayal about what girls need and want? How do these messages make you feel? Why might being treated like a weak child be appealing to some girls and women? What might be some of the outcomes for a woman in a long-term relationship in which her partner treats her like a child? What might be some of the outcomes for the man is such a relationship?

Thirst

1. Throughout the novels until Bella becomes a vampire, she is "forbidden fruit" for Edward. She tries many times to have sex with Edward, and her blood "sings" for him, but he resists

her. That is, Edward controls the intimacy in their relationship. What messages about gender are embedded in this narrative?

2. As you read through the main ways that Christians have interpreted the story of Adam and Eve and the forbidden fruit, what were the roles, gifts, strengths, and weaknesses of the man and woman in each version?

3. As you read through Genesis 1–3, what does the text actually say about the roles, gifts, strengths, and weaknesses of the man and woman?

4. How do Meyer's interpretations of Genesis via Twilight reinforce negative stereotypes about men, women, and sexuality?

5. What did you learn about eros in this chapter, both in the context of sexuality and in life in general? In what ways do you see eros in the relationship between Edward and Bella?

Born Again

1. What are some examples of how Bella, Edward, and Carlisle function as saviors in the story?

2. In what ways do women and girls function as healthy and unhealthy "saviors" in our culture? What about men and boys?

3. When Bella becomes pregnant with Renesmee, Edward and Carlisle both initially want her to have an abortion. What do you believe about abortion? If a pregnant woman is in danger of death because of the pregnancy, who do you think should be involved in the decision about whether to end the pregnancy? What does the phrase "sanctity of life" mean to you?

4. Edward, Bella, and Carlisle represent a generation of young adults who describe themselves as "spiritual but not religious." What does this phrase mean? Why has the word "religious" developed negative connotations for so many people today?

Golden Eyes and Granite Flesh

1. Before she becomes a vampire, Bella sometimes worries that she won't be attractive enough to "hold Edward" after she is changed. She worries that the absence of her fragrant blood

will make him lose interest in her and that she won't be able to feel as much emotional and physical longing for him as she does in her human form. Do any of these anxieties feel familiar to you? How does anxiety over keeping a partner's approval both form and deform women and men?

2. How do you think genuinely living in the kingdom of heaven might affect our understanding of gender and sex?

3. The Cullens' golden eyes represent their daily choice to exercise self-control and self-denial in order to contribute to the common good of their human neighbors. They are a spiritual community in this way, practicing a common (though hidden) form of discipline in order to love their neighbors. What are some common spiritual practices that might help a Christian community to more effectively love and serve its neighbors in "hidden" ways? Why might "hidden" service be especially important in our day?

4. After she is married and pregnant, Bella realizes that something bigger than her relationship with Edward is unfolding. The dreams, the visions, and the amazing fact of the supernatural all around her begin to convince her that she inhabits a larger story that is going somewhere. She says to Jacob, "I guess you could call it faith" (*Breaking Dawn*, 190). Where in your life have you seen signs that something bigger than just your life is unfolding?

Those Who Must Be Obeyed

1. In what ways do the Volturi represent religious institutions that are corrupted by power?

2. In what ways are the Volturi stereotypes of masculinity and femininity in our culture? The ancient Volturi wives have never left the towers of Volterra, do not have names, and for all intents and purposes are nonentities. What kinds of cultural stereotypes about elderly women are contained in this characterization? Do you know older women who are like the Volturi wives? Discuss some of the older women you know who do not fit these stereotypes.

3. The Volturi colonize other vampires by controlling the size of

other covens and use violence and deceit to collect vampires with special powers. What are the forms of colonization that are taking place now in the world? How might the church resist colonization in the world?

Engaging the Powers

1. In what ways does Bella become the premier agent of reconciliation in this story? What can Christians learn from Bella and Carlisle about fostering reconciliation in the world?
2. Bella refuses to demonize vampires or werewolves, and she calls out Edward and Jacob when they demonize one another. Who are some of the groups that are demonized in our culture? By the church? What can we learn from Bella and Carlisle that can help us resist this kind of demonization?
3. How has Twilight shaped your theological imagination?

Acknowledgments

First I want to thank my daughters, Holly and Jeanette, for prodding me into reading *Twilight*. Well, for prodding me into doing lots of things, including white-water rafting, eating sushi, and in general, having more fun. I'm also grateful to Randy for being so patient and forgiving as I hole up to read, think, and write. My research assistants, Mireya Martinez and Shellie Ross, have been angels, helping with all kinds of little details along the way. What wonderful colleagues I have, too, who have often asked how the vampire book is coming along and wished me well, especially John Holbert, Michael Hawn, Jamie Clark-Soles, and Beka Miles. I think that my editor, Jana Riess, is amazing in her ability to be both ruthless and encouraging as she scrutinizes every word in the manuscript. She truly calls forth the best from writers. I'm grateful for all the other wonderful people on the WJK editorial team who helped with typesetting, cover design, and the rest.

Finally I want to thank Stephenie Meyer for writing her dream. Even when I disagree with her, even when I want to throw the books across the room because the gender problems make me crazy, I am grateful. Stephenie Meyer defies stereotypes about what a "housewife and mom" can and cannot do. She has created a pop culture phenomenon that in many ways captures the spiritual questions and longings of this generation. May more of us have her courage to follow our dreams.

Notes

Introduction

1. http://twilightseriestheories.com/index.php/2009/05/07/press-release-fall
-2009-twilight-saga-publishing-program/, accessed August 3, 2009.

2. Domestic and foreign box office receipts for all of the films are available
at http://boxofficemojo.com/movies/?id=twilight08.htm.

3. The editions of the books that I used were *Twilight*, First Media Tie-in
Edition (New York: Little, Brown & Co., Megan Tingley Books, 2008); *New
Moon*, First Paperback Edition (New York: Little, Brown & Co., Megan Tingley
Books,: 2008); *Eclipse* (New York: Little, Brown, & Co., 2006); and *Breaking
Dawn* (New York: Little, Brown, & Co., 2008).

Chapter 1: The Good Family

1. Interestingly, both Esme and Rosalie had been victims of violence at
the hands of their intimate partners. Alice, too, was a victim of family violence
while human because of her gift of precognition. Her family cruelly put her in
an asylum where a vampire later changed her. Bella, who eventually becomes a
member of the Cullen family, also suffers violence, but at the hands of vampires:
James, Edward, and unborn Renesmee. She narrowly escapes becoming a victim of sexual violence when human thugs descend upon her in the town of Port
Angeles. Violence against women is an undercurrent throughout the series and is
even more pronounced in Meyer's stand-alone novel *The Host*.

2. Focus on the Family is an evangelical organization devoted to nurturing
Christian families and marriages according to the vision of its founder, James
Dobson. http://www.focusonthefamily.com/.

3. For a quick and enjoyable primer on Latter-day Saint history, theology,
and practices, see Jana Riess and Christopher Kimball Bigelow, *Mormonism for
Dummies* (Hoboken, NJ: Wiley Publishing, Inc., 2005).

4. H. Davis Farnsworth, "Vampire Families Are Forever," *Sunstone* (December, 2009): 31–37.

5. Beth Felker Jones, *Touched by a Vampire: Discovering the Hidden Messages in the Twilight Saga* (Colorado Springs, Co: Multnomah, 2009), 9.

6. Ibid., 88–96.

7. Riess and Bigelow, *Mormonism*, 337.

Chapter 2: I'm Only Half of Me

1. I say immortal, but in fact vampires can be killed with some effort. In *Twilight* they have to be torn to pieces, and then the pieces have to be burned into ashes. Since their bodies are hard as granite, only three things can kill vampires: other vampires, werewolves, or possibly a nuclear holocaust.

2. Eric W. Jepson, "Saturday's Werewolf: Twilight, Monsters, and Mormons," *Sunstone* 157 (December 2009): 24.

3. Ibid.

4. Jana Riess and Christopher Kimball Bigelow, *Mormonism for Dummies* (Hoboken, NJ: Wiley Publishing, Inc., 2005), 37.

5. To be fair, women sometimes abuse men, and in same-sex relationships you can also find abuse. However, since this book is about Edward and Bella, and the vast majority of readers are young women, I am writing about the abusive partner as "he." Also, more than 90 percent of domestic violence in the real world is male against female. For statistics and more resources on domestic violence see www.faithtrustinstitute.org.

6. For more information about what constitutes domestic violence, see the National Coalition Against Domestic Violence, "The Problem" at http://www.ncadv.org/learn/TheProblem.php.

7. Just three of the many references to Edward's reckless driving are found in *Twilight*, 179, 181, and 202.

8. These characteristics are as follows: fails to conform to social norms, as indicated by frequently performing illegal acts and pursuing illegal occupations; is deceitful and manipulative of others; is impulsive, holding a succession of jobs or residences; is irritable or aggressive, engaging in physical fights; exhibits reckless disregard for the safety of self or others, misusing motor vehicles, or playing with fire; is consistently irresponsible, failing to find or sustain work or to pay bills or debts; demonstrates lack of remorse for the harm his or her behavior causes others. Susan Vaught, "A Very Dangerous Boy," in *A New Dawn: Your Favorite Authors on Stephenie Meyer's Twilight Series*, ed. Ellen Hopkins (Dallas: BenBella Books, 2008), 1–13.

9. Dave Roberts, *The Twilight Gospel: The Spiritual Roots of Stephenie Meyer's Vampire Saga* (Oxford: Monarch, 2009), 99.

10. Ibid., 120.

11. Christine Wicker, "Barna Survey: Baptists Have Highest Divorce Rate" in *Dallas Morning News*; reprinted at www.adherents.com/largecom/baptist_divorce.html (accessed July 14, 2010).

12. Beth Felker Jones, *Touched by a Vampire: Discovering the Hidden Messages in the Twilight Saga* (Colorado Springs: Multnomah, 2009), 107–10.

13. Ibid., 25.

Chapter 3: Is Twilight Bad News for Girls?

1. Mary Pipher, *Reviving Ophelia: Saving the Selves of Adolescent Girls* (New York: Putnam, 1994).

2. For an excellent study of why young women cut themselves and what it takes to heal, see Marilee Strong, *A Bright Red Scream: Self-Mutilation and the Language of Pain* (New York: Penguin, 1999).

3. The extent of Victoria's exploitation of Riley is detailed in Meyer's subsequent novella, *The Short Second Life of Bree Tanner* (Boston: Little, Brown, 2010).

Chapter 4: Thirst

1. I say "mother" because this is the usual primary caregiver in our early days. For some of us the loving caregiver was a father, grandmother, or nanny. Regardless of who she or he was, when we were newborns, we were thirsty, and we bonded with the one who slaked our thirst.

2. Roger Shuler, "Techniques of Touch: New Knowledge about Nurturing Newborns," *UAB Magazine*, vol. 21, no. 2 (Summer 2001), http://main.uab.edu/show.asp?durki=41209, accessed May 3, 2010.

3. Sandra L. Gravett, *From Twilight to Breaking Dawn: Religious Themes in the Twilight Saga* (Danvers, MA: Chalice Press, 2010), 31.

4. Jana Riess and Christopher Kimball Bigelow, *Mormonism for Dummies* (Hoboken, NJ: Wiley Publishing, Inc., 2005), 28.

5. See Elaine Heath, *The Mystic Way of Evangelism: A Contemplative Vision for Christian Outreach* (Grand Rapids: Baker Academic), 52–58.

Chapter 5: Born Again

1. Dave Roberts, *The Twilight Gospel: The Spiritual Roots of Stephenie Meyer's Vampire Saga* (Oxford: Monarch, 2009),120.

2. Ibid., 153–54.

3. Kurt Bruner, *The Twilight Phenomenon: Forbidden Fruit or Thirst-Quenching Fantasy?* (Shippensburg, PA: Destiny Image Publishers, 2009), 15.

4. Ibid., 16–17.

5. Ibid., 17.

6. Sandra L. Gravett, *From Twilight to Breaking Dawn: Religious Themes in the Twilight Saga* (Danvers, MA: Chalice Press, 2010), 39.

7. Kurt Bruner catalogues the monstrous behavior of both mythic vampires from stories around the world and real sadists upon whose atrocities some of the modern vampire stories such as *Dracula* were taken (*Twilight Phenomenon*, 55–79).

8. Miroslav Volf, *Exclusion and Embrace* (Nashville: Abingdon Press, 1996).

9. The third rule in Wesley's three General Rules is "attend to all the ordinances of God," which means to be faithful to all the spiritual practices, including

worship, Bible reading, fasting, communion, and the like. For more on Wesley's General Rules see Kevin Watson, *A Blueprint for Discipleship* (Nashville: Discipleship Resources, 2009).

10. Gravett, *From Twilight*, 49.

11. http://www.absolutelyrics.com/lyrics/view/john_lennon/give_peace_a _chance/, accessed May 21, 2010.

12. Edward Hicks, "The Peaceable Kingdom," http://en.wikipedia.org/wiki/ Edward_Hicks, accessed May 21, 2010.

13. The preface version of the event is more introspective about Bella's impending sacrificial death than is the event as recorded at the end of the novel, 444–52. Her decision to die for her mother is found on p. 430.

14. The traditional Apostles' Creed states that Jesus "was crucified, dead, and buried: he descended into hell; the third day he rose again from the dead." "The Apostle's Creed, Traditional Version," *The United Methodist Hymnal* (Nashville: The United Methodist Publishing House, 1989), 881.

Chapter 6: Golden Eyes and Granite Flesh

1. Lynn Anderson, "Put Your Hand in the Hand," http://www.cowboylyrics .com/lyrics/anderson-lynn/put-your-hand-in-the-hand-275.html, accessed May 26, 2010.

2. Kinnaman and Lyons focus on how the church, Christians, and Jesus look through the eyes of sixteen-to-twenty-nine-year-old people outside the church. David Kinnaman and Gabe Lyons, *UnChristian: What a New Generation Thinks about Christianity . . . and Why It Matters* (Grand Rapids: Baker, 2007).

3. *Lord Save Us*, http://lordsaveusthemovie.com/theater.html; *The Invention of Lying*, http://www.imdb.com/title/tt1058017/; *Religulous*, http://www .imdb.com/title/tt0815241/; *Saved*, http://www.imdb.com/title/tt0332375/; *Jesus Camp*, http://www.imdb.com/title/tt0486358/; accessed May 26, 2010.

4. The phrase "kingdom of heaven" and "kingdom of God" in the New Testament mean the same thing. Some feminist theologians prefer using the term "kin-dom of God" because it connotes relationship without patriarchy or any of the vestiges of imperialism. Other theologians use the term "reign of God" to maintain a sense of God's authority while removing patriarchal imagery.

5. "The Butterfly Effect," http://en.wikipedia.org/wiki/Butterfly_effect, accessed June 7, 2010.

6. To learn more about process theology see Jay B. McDaniel and Donna Bowman, eds., *A Handbook to Process Theology* (St. Louis: Chalice Press, 2006). A good introduction to open theism is Gregory Boyd, *The God of the Possible: A Biblical Introduction to the Open View of God* (Grand Rapids: Baker, 2000).

7. Kurt Bruner, *The Twilight Phenomenon: Forbidden Fruit or Thirst-Quenching Fantasy?* (Shippensburg, PA: Destiny Image Publishers, 2009), 139.

8. Ibid., 142–43.

9. Dave Roberts, *The Twilight Gospel: The Spiritual Roots of Stephenie Meyer's Vampire Saga* (Oxford: Monarch, 2009), 113.

10. Ibid., 114.

11. Tyler Chadwick, "Why Twilight is Good for You: How the Uncanny Can Make Us More Christ-Like," *Sunstone* (December, 2009): 49.

12. *The Matrix*, http://www.imdb.com/title/tt0133093/, accessed June 7, 2010.

Chapter 7: Those Who Must Be Obeyed

1. Sandra L. Gravett, *From Twilight to Breaking Dawn: Religious Themes in the Twilight Saga* (Danvers, MA: Chalice Press, 2010), 90.

2. In *New Moon* Alice says that vampires usually live alone or with a mate (428), but here we encounter a history of covens from which the Volturi would harvest one member with special gifts and then destroy the rest of the coven (*Breaking Dawn*, 601–2).

3. Gravett, *From Twlight*, 93.

Chapter 8: Engaging the Powers

1. Dave Roberts, *The Twilight Gospel: The Spiritual Roots of Stephenie Meyer's Vampire Saga* (Oxford: Monarch, 2009). By now it will not surprise you that Roberts approaches this topic by looking in the Bible to see what it says about the undead. Failing to find literal vampires or werewolves there, he moves on to the witch of Endor, a medium through whom King Saul makes contact with the spirit of Samuel, who is dead but whose immortal spirit is still alive. The story of the Gerasene demoniac (Mark 5:1–20) would have served Roberts better, connecting the man's insanity and deterioration with the tortured condition of those bitten by the undead. The demon-possessed man even lives in the tombs, a typical hideout for vampires in many a horror film.

2. Rebecca Housel, "The Tao of Jacob," in *Twilight and Philosophy: Vampires, Vegetarians, and the Pursuit of Immortality* (New York: John Wiley & Sons, 2009), 243.

3. Sandra L. Gravett, *From Twilight to Breaking Dawn: Religious Themes in the Twilight Saga* (Danvers, MA: Chalice Press, 2010), 94–95.

4. Brian D. McLaren, *A New Kind of Christianity: Ten Questions That Are Transforming the Faith* (New York: HarperOne, 2010), 257.

Index

abortion, 72, 82

abuse of women. *See* violence against women

Acts, book of, 86–87, 99

Adam and Eve, xii–xiii, 34, 54, 57–64

adult children of alcoholics, 16

agape, 65

alcoholism, 14, 16

Alec, 108, 109

Alice

  Aro as covetous for rare power of, 114, 115

  Bella's relationship with, 47, 128

  and Bella's relationship with were-wolves, 40

  Bella's wedding and, 43

  clairvoyance of, 45, 79, 96, 100, 114, 119, 141n1

  conversion of, to a vampire, 97

  in Cullen family, 4

  disappearance of, 47

  marriage of, 4, 18

  as materialistic Cosmo girl, 14, 45

  protection of Bella by, 29–30, 81

  as victim of violence, 141n1

  on Volturi, 108–9

Anabaptists, 118

androgyny, 21, 46

Angela, 18, 128

angels, 106–7, 108

anger. *See* rage and domestic violence

antisocial personality disorder, 32, 70, 142n8

Apostles' Creed, 144n14

armies of newborn vampires, 41–42, 46, 68, 81–82, 110–12, 129

Aro

  age of, 108

  angelic appearance of, 108

  as collector of rare things, 109, 112, 115

  as covetous of Alice's rare powers, 114, 115

  destruction of immortal children by, 112, 113

  and enmity between Cullen family and Volturi, 114–16

  eyes of, 110

  group living situation of, 108

  as leader of Volturi, 108–10, 115

  on love between Bella and Edward, 65

  on problems of Western cultures, 102

Bella's inadequacy in, 37
Bella's insecurity in, 43
Carlisle in, 75, 76, 104
Carlisle on Edward's goodness in,
94
Charlie's criticism of Bella in, 102
Edward on evil nature of vampires
in, 71
Edward on salvation in, 72, 93
Edward's disappearance in, 56
Edward's fear of Bella's drowning,
34
Edward's self-denying love for
Bella, 65
family in, 9–10
Jacob Black in, 39–41, 56, 128
Jasper's attempted attack on Bella
in, 10
Sam and his friends in, 127
self-destructive impulse of Bella in,
38–41
on vampires living alone with a
mate, 145n2
Volturi in, 108–9
See also Twilight series
New Testament. *See* Jesus Christ;
*and specific New Testament
books*
Nicodemus, 85

Old Testament. *See specific Old Testament books*
open theism, 96
original sin, 59–60

parables
of Good Samaritan, 11, 88
of kingdom of heaven, 94–95
paternalism. *See* gender role stereotypes

Paul
exorcism by, 99
on power of God, 97
on reconciliation, 88, 123
on resurrected body, 90, 91
on singleness, 35
on will power, 97
peace, 79–80, 88, 100, 102, 112, 117.
See also reconciliation
pedophilia, 20–21
Pentecost, 86–87, 88, 100–101
Pentecostals, 122
perichoresis (circle dance), 67
Peter, First Letter by, 83
Philippians, Letter to, 64
physical abuse of women. *See* violence against women
Pipher, Mary, 38
Plato, xiv
pornography, 65
postmodern culture, 69–70
posttraumatic stress, 112
process theology, 96
Protestant Christianity
afterlife and, 90
interpretation of Genesis narrative
by, 59–60, 63
open theism in, 96
process theology in, 96
on salvation, 96
Proverbs, book of, 48–49

Quil, 20
Quileutes. *See* werewolves/Quileutes

rage and domestic violence, 25–29, 31
rape. *See* sexual assault; violence
against women
reconciliation
Bella's role in, 79, 80, 124, 127–32

after her conversion to a vampire, 36, 47–49, 83, 84, 89–91, 100
compared with Harry Potter series, xiii, 122
coupling and marriage in, 18–35
Cullen family as exemplary in, 3–7, 10–14, 17, 102, 106, 117, 119, 131–32
damaged family in, 7–11, 15–17
dangers of romance between Edward and Bella in, 22–44
desire in, xv, 53, 55–56, 62–68
divorce in, 7–10, 15–17, 123
eros and ecstasy in, 65–68
escape theme in, 38–42
forbidden fruit in, 55–56, 62–65, 68
gender role stereotypes in, 36–49
meadow scene of, xi, xii, 26–27
Mormon messages in, 6–7, 16, 21–22, 90, 95–96, 103
plot summary of, x–xi
publication of, x–xi
reconciliation in, 79–81, 83, 88, 121–33
sales and popularity of, ix–xii, 65
salvation in, 89–91, 93–94, 96–105
self-sacrifice of Bella in, xiii, 41–42, 68, 78–82, 144n13
sexual passion in, 28, 33, 56, 63–68
sin as concept in, 69–71
singleness in, 8–9, 18, 21–22, 34
theological themes of generally, xiii–xv, 133
translations of, 36, 65
true love theme in, 65–68
violence against women in, xiii, 21, 23–34, 141n1
See also vampires; Volturi; were-

wolves/Quileutes; *and specific characters and specific books in series*

vampires
armies of newborn vampires, 41–42, 46, 68, 81–82, 110–12, 129
Bella as "shield" among, 83, 100, 117, 119, 131
Bella's conversion to, 43, 47–49, 68, 82–83, 89–91, 95, 100
Bella's desire to be changed into vampire, 27, 56, 89
conflicts among, 79
creation of family by, 4, 77
Cullen family as exemplary family, 3–7, 10–14, 17, 102, 106, 117, 119, 131–32
desire of victims for, xv
enmity between werewolves and, 79–80, 101–2, 126–28
evil nature and sin of, 71–72, 74, 93, 121–22
gender role stereotypes of, 44–46
God's mercy and forgiveness for, 76, 77
immortal children and, 112–13
killing of, 142n1
mating of, for life, 6, 18–19, 145n2
monstrous behavior of, 143n7
reconciliation between werewolves and, 80, 88, 123–24, 126, 128–32
red eyes of, from drinking human blood, 97
sadism of female vampires, 46
smell of, 126–27, 130
special gifts of, 99–101
traditional stories on, 121–22, 123

Romanians versus, 110, 115–16,
119, 125
St. Marcus and, 109, 118–19
Southern Wars and, 110–12, 114
violence and terrorism by, 109–13,
116, 118, 145n2
witnesses for, 116–17
wives of, 46, 108, 113

werewolves/Quileutes
androgyny of Leah, 21, 46
Edward's claim of protecting Bella
from, 30
enmity between vampires and,
79–80, 101–2, 126–28
enmity between Volturi and, 119,
126
female werewolves, 21–22, 46
imprinting and coupling by, 19–22,
34, 56, 80, 131
Jacob Black as, 19, 30, 39–41
Native American beliefs of, 70
origins of, 126

reconciliation between vampires
and, 80, 88, 123–24, 126, 128–
32
Sam's injury of girlfriend Emily,
21, 46
self-sacrifice of Quileute woman
and legend of the Cold Ones,
41–42, 81, 126
as shape-shifters, 126
smell of, 127
traditional stories of werewolves,
121–22, 123
Wesley, John, 77, 144n9
Wisdom figure, 48
wise woman of Proverbs, 48–49
witch of Endor, 145n1
witnesses, 86–87, 88, 116–17
Wizard of Oz, The, 70
women. See feminists; gender role
stereotypes; violence against
women; *and specific female
characters*